CONNECT & CONVEY

Dr. Ruchi Tandon

Asst. Professor

Amity Institute of Corporate Communication

Amity University, Noida.

&

Dr. Lalit Kumar Yadav

Asst. Professor

Amity Institute of Corporate Communication

Amity University, Noida.

Published by

Notion Press Media Pvt. Ltd.

50, Chettiyar Agaram Main Road, Vanagaram, Chennai,

Tamil Nadu 600095

Printed by

Notion Press Media Pvt. Ltd.

50, Chettiyar Agaram Main Road, Vanagaram, Chennai,

Tamil Nadu 600095

ISBN	:	**979-8894464893**
Published on	:	**14 June 2024**
Edition	:	**First**
Price	:	**399.00 INR**

ACKNOWLEDGEMENT

Jai Shri Bala Ji

On the very outset of this book I would like to extend my sincere & heartfelt obligation towards almighty God who helped me in this endeavor.

I also acknowledge with a deep sense of reverence, gratitude towards my parents who have always inspired me by all means.

At last but not least gratitude goes to all of my friends who directly or indirectly helped me to complete this book.

Any omission in this brief acknowledgement does not mean lack of gratitude.

Thanking you

Table of Contents

Unit 1

FUNDAMENTALS OF COMMUNICATION

GOALS

After studying this unit you should be able to:

- Recognize the function of business communication in companies;
- Examine the critical elements of corporate communication;
- Through a case study, get an understanding of the verbal and nonverbal communication styles of characters.

STRUCTURE

1.1 Overview

1.2 Evolution of Communication

1.3 Communication Elements

1.4 Distinguishing Business from General Communication

1.5 Business Communication's Objective

1.6 A Case Study of the Profile of an Effective Communicator

1.7 The "Attitude of You"

1.8 Key Aspects of Business Communication

1.9 Using appropriate language

1.10 7 C's of Communication

1.1 OVERVIEW

We are all aware that IR 5.0 has changed the world around us. Industry 5.0, the New Education Policy 2020, and other agencies have also emphasized the need for effective communication skills. In today's VUCA world, everyone is engaged in marketing or branding. To survive, we need to prove ourselves. We must imagine that we are always on stage, whether we are speaking or not. We need to survive in both our professional and social lives. This is not possible without effective communication skills. Communication skills are very important for all of us. They are a buzzword. They are everywhere. They are a lifelong process. In a nutshell, communication skills are essential life skills that will help us navigate various situations in our professional and personal lives. Mastering this one skill guarantees that you will reach the zenith of success.

The ability to communicate is one of the most important skills. It's critical to comprehend the subtleties of communication. This unit's topics will include how dialogue has developed into its current state. We will research the distinctions between commercial and general communication.

We are aware of the significance of communication within an organization. In a corporate setting, we communicate with managers, employees, and subordinates through various means such as emails, letters, business reports, and proposals. We also engage in one-on-one conversations, phone calls, and intercom communications. The exchange of information is the unifying factor in all these activities.

Without effective communication, no organization or company can operate smoothly. Communication is at the heart of every enterprise's actions. The better our ability to communicate, the more likely we are to succeed. An understanding of commercial principles and levels is of little use in a functional setting without appropriate communication. For instance, if a candidate cannot effectively convey their views and ideas to interviewers, even with an outstanding academic record, they may not succeed in a placement interview. Most successful business owners and managers possess exceptional communication skills.

1.2 EVOLUTION OF COMMUNICATION

One method of engaging with people is through communication, which is essential to our existence. Proper comprehension follows from effective communication. Over the years, or perhaps I should say ages, communication tactics have evolved and continue to do so. This section will examine the evolution of communication, highlighting that talking to each other is a process involving the exchange of words or signs to convey a message. We encounter various forms of communication daily, whether it be speaking, writing, or listening. To deliver a message clearly, good communication is crucial. There are different forms of communication, including spoken and unspoken. In Unit 3, we will explore these in more detail. For now, let's examine the evolution of communication in its current form.

Cave drawings

Humans have been communicating in various ways for ages. Cave paintings represent one of the earliest forms of human communication. These paintings are not merely artistic; they recorded significant events, marked boundaries, and conveyed specific messages through symbols.

Symbolic Communication

Our predecessors used various signs and symbols to communicate. Around 10,000 B.C., rock engravings known as petroglyphs were created. These engravings on stones depicted various accounts. Later, ideograms such as numbers were developed. The creation of characters and, eventually, alphabets marked a significant turning point in the history of communication.

Signals of Smoke

In the past, people used objects to communicate. One method of sending messages was through smoke signals.

Carriers Pigeons

One widely used technique for communicating written messages involved using pigeons as messengers. Carrier pigeons played a significant role in both World Wars I and II, functioning as a kind of "postal service."

The postal system

Egyptians employed courier services in the past to send the official eight directives. Rome, China, India, and Persia all possessed sophisticated mail systems. The first paid envelope delivery service and postal box system were implemented in Paris in the year   1653.

Printing Press

The Germans invented the first printing press in 1440, which drastically altered the nature of communication. The first newspapers appeared in the sixteenth century.

Sound system/Radio

A significant change in print communication technology occurred with the emergence of wireless power as a means of message transmission in 1893, leading to the advent of radio transmission.

Telegram

Long-distance communication was revolutionized by the telegraph. Samuel Morse invented Morse code, using sequences of clicks, tones, and lights to convey messages. The first telegraph message was transmitted in 1844

Phone

The invention of the telephone quickly made it the most popular and reliable means of spoken communication.

Television

Television followed, becoming as integral to our lives as the telephone. It serves as a form of indirect communication.

Online Communication

Computers, which became widely available in the 1950s, are now a primary means of communication. This led to significant technological advancements in the communication process. The term "Internet" first appeared in 1973 and is now one of the most commonly used terms.

Email

Electronic mails, or emails, have become essential tools for communication in both personal and professional contexts.

SMS

Text messaging is another quick and efficient form of communication that utilizes data networks.

Social Networks

The most recent form of communication, social media, has digitized everything. It has expanded the global community and became one of the most frequently used methods of communication during the pandemic.

Over the decades, communication has undergone numerous changes. Today, communication is more efficient and convenient than ever before.

Activity 1

Consider how you typically communicate with others. Name any three modes of communication which you use frequently.

a) ……………………………

b) ……………………………

c) ……………………………

1.3 COMMUNICATION ELEMENTS

During Activity 1, you mentioned three different modes of communication that you frequently use. Now, evaluate whether each time you spoke, it was efficient and conveyed an appropriate or suitable message. The response will most likely be "No." This highlights the importance of understanding communication and identifying which forms are most effective

Definition

According to Mary Ellen Guffey, "Communication is the transmission of information and meaning from one individual or group to another". Fundamental components of communication are as follows:

- Source
- Message
- Channels
- Receiver
- The surroundings
- Context
- Interference

These components come together to produce the entire communication process, which Unit 2 will cover in detail.

1.4 DISTINGUISHING BUSINESS COMMUNICATION FROM GENERAL COMMUNICATION

As we can see, communication involves the exchange of information from one person to another. When we discuss business communication, it pertains to business-related domains and subjects. It stems from general communication but focuses specifically on business activities. General communication covers daily or broad topics that may not be specific in nature. The primary difference between the two lies in the context and focus of the communication.

The type of communication between the two is what separates them.

Table 1 illustrates how the two differ from one another.

	Business Communication	**General Communication**
Format	It uses a specific format forcommunication.	It uses varied formats forcommunication.
Category	It is usually formal in nature.	It involves personal touch.
Extent/Reach	It usually is practical & unbiased.	It can be vast and can be fictitious and biased, at times.
Demonstration/ Presentation	It specifically follows the norms and procedures of the organization.	It is informal and different methods can be used.
Aim/Intention	It focuses on the aim of theorganization.	It lacks focus.
Kind/ Nature/Pattern	It is official in nature.	It is personal in nature.
Feedback	This requires feedback.	May not be required

Table 1: Comparing Business Communication and General Communication

Activity 2

Classify the following as correspondence for business or general use:

a) Communicating the attrition report to the HR Manager.

b) Conflict arises from inadequate communication.

c) The policies and guidelines that must be adhered to throughout regular operations are communicated by top management.

d) It appears that she struggles with communicating.

………………………………………………………………………………

………………………………………………………………………………

………………………………………………………………………………

………………………………………………………………………………

1.5 BUSINESS COMMUNICATION'S OBJECTIVE

An organization's development or success can be gauged by its communication. Every managerial or administrative task requires communication, whether it is interacting, arranging, recruiting, organizing, coordinating, or making decisions.

Gaining proficiency in these areas is necessary to engage effectively in the communication process. Participation involves developing skills in gathering, compiling, arranging, evaluating, and assessing facts, understanding the distinction between facts and conclusions, and proficient communication.

Successful communication only occurs when the goal is achieved. The goal of communication may be to motivate, persuade, or inform, resulting in a desired action. Every scenario aims to bring about a beneficial change in the listener or recipient, such as a shift in attitude, perception, or belief. Therefore, all corporate communication is ultimately manipulative, purposeful, and goal-driven. Consequently, the measure of communication effectiveness is based on how well the ultimate objective is accomplished.

1.6 A Case Study of the Profile of an Effective Communicator

Now, using a case study, let's examine the characteristics of a good communicator.

The Case of the Less Expensive Customer

[Sunday: 1 p.m. Fitwell Shoes' storefront in Phoenix Mall! A box of Fitwell shoes is held by Mr. and Mrs. X as they enter. Mr. X works for a global corporation as a vice president. He is decked up in sandals, olive green bermudas, and a bright orange T-shirt. Mrs. X had on a pale pink saree. She's carrying a little handbag and a shopping bag. Mrs. X stops outside to window shop, and Mr. X enters the store first. Mr. A, a young trainee sales executive sent for training from headquarters, greets him as soon as he enters the store.]

Mr. A: Hi, sir! Good morning! In what way may I assist you?

Mr. X: I feel like these shoes are seconds because I got them last Sunday and have only worn them once. (Tries to hand over the package to Mr. A, who has his hands behind his back)

Mr. A: This showroom is not equipped with seconds, sir.

Mr. X: (unwrapping the shoe box) It hit me right away, although I liked the color and may have missed it. The two sneakers' stripes are not the same. It appears to be an error in manufacture.

Mr. A: (Keeping his hands behind his back while glancing at the shoes). This is how they are intended, sir. It's not a flaw in the manufacture.

Mr. X: This can't be the design (trying to get the shoes to Mr. A so he may look them over). It seems to be a "seconds" pair and is really an alignment problem.

Mr. A: I can show you other pairs as well, sir (still not taking the pair). They are all designed in the same manner. After asking a store employee to fetch a few pairs of the same manufacture, he leaves to serve other customers; when he comes back in around five minutes, he discovers Mr. X trying on another pair. Remember, I stated they are all created in the same manner. It's not a manufacturing flaw; rather, it's the design.
Mr. X: Then it seems to me that this dealership is selling faulty merchandise. They come from old stock.

Mr. A: As a rule, we don't maintain any "seconds" in the showroom, as I already informed you. We actually don't have a lot of "seconds" inventory due of our most advanced production line.

Mr. X: Alright, I want to return these. (Grasping up his pair of shoes). I don't want to use a pair that is broken. You then inform me that I am unable to return it. Which type of store is this?

Mr. A: (saying calmly but with a gloomy expression) Sir, I assured you that they are not flawed. Furthermore, you've previously utilized them. How can I retrieve them?

[At this point, Mr. G, the showroom manager, emerges from his cabin, sees them, and approaches Mr. X]

Mr. G: May I help you, sir?

Mr. A: Let me introduce myself. (Aiming to present Mr. X.)

Mr. X: (Interrupting Mr. A) My name is Mr. X, and I purchased these shoes from your showroom last week (showing them to him). Something about the design bothers me, in my opinion (points at the toes). It was really brought up by a few of my pals.

Mr. G: Were you aware of this when you purchased them? Mr. X: I observed this, but it didn't really upset me.

Mr. G: How come?

Mr. X: Perhaps I was focused on the color.

Mr. G: Alright, Mr. X, there isn't a manufacturing or design flaw in this. Conversely, this is how they are intended to seem. They all follow the same pattern, as you can see (pointing to the pairs that are on the ground).
Mr. X: They appear aged. Furthermore, I don't want to dress in anything that appears cheap.

Mr. G: It is not our policy to...

Mr. X: (cutting him off) Alright, I'm leaving them right here (plopping the two down on the ground). Kindly use them anyway you see fit.

Mr. G: (seeing down at the two for a long time) Are you in possession of a receipt?

Mr. X: (Gesturing about in the shoe box and wallet for a moment). Allow me to verify with my spouse (while turning to face her; she is approaching them). Are you in possession of the shoes' receipt?

Mrs. X: No, I don't believe you handed it to me (as she begins to go through her handbag).

Mr. X: I have no idea. I might have brought it home. Kindly let us a minute, Mr. G. (and ask Mr. A to go with him to his cabin). What are they saying, Mrs. X?

Mr. X: Returning sold products is not part of their policy.

Mrs. X: They won't accept them back, as I have stated.

Mr. X: Is it correct? They'll need to return them.

[In the meanwhile, Mr. A approaches Mr. X by coming out from behind the store]

Mr. A: You know, we'll need to confirm this with our central office. Two days may pass before you find out.

Mr. X: On weekdays, I'm unable to come.

Mr. A: So, Sunday of next week?

Mr. X: However, on Sunday I have other commitments.

Mr. A: Then you may call and find out (handing him a card with his phone number on it).

Mr. X: (pulling his own business card out of his wallet and giving it to Mr. A instead of taking the card) Why don't you tell me?

Mr A: We certainly will. However, if we are unable to reach you, you may also attempt.

Mr. X: (With reluctance) All right, (takes the card and walks away).

Mr. A: (removing the two from the ground). While you wait, you are welcome to keep them with you.

Mr. X: (Stepping back in his direction). How am I going to handle them?

Mr. A: Sir, I am unable to detain them here until I receive word from our central office. Secondly, they might get lost if there is no receipt.

Mr. X: (glaring at him intently and pausing to reflect) Alright. but please inform me right now.

Mr. A: (repackaging the pair in their box and giving it to him) Okay.

[On advice of Mr. G, the next day, Mr. A speaks to Mr. , General Manager of the headquarters. Mr. V asks him to fax the details. Mr. A sends the following communication.]

Dear, Sir

Mr. X, a client, wishes to return a pair of shoes that he purchased a week ago from the showroom. He asserts that the design has a manufacturing flaw. He's actually saying that we're selling seconds from this store. Mr. G and I made futile attempts to persuade him of our ideas. Finally, we assured him that we would inform him of our decision only after speaking with head office, so as to avoid his making a spectacle. I've also been effective in persuading him to return with the duo. However, he will undoubtedly expect our response in a few days. Kindly let me know.

With regards,

Mr. A [On Monday, the next day, Mr. A departs the town on an official visit. Mr. G discovers the following communication from Mr. V on the fax machine on Tuesday morning.]

"Salute him, give him a new pair, and don't ask questions if he is a

₹ 4500/-customer. However, make it very apparent to him that it is not feasible if he is a ₹ 1250/-customer.

Please keep in mind that although the customer is king, kings can also be huge, little, wealthy, or impoverished.

Which communicator in this case study is the most effective? And why?

The majority of readers would say that Mr. A is the best communicator. Why?

Mr. A is a persuasive, courteous, composed, adaptable, astute, and professional salesman who utilizes appropriate body language, offers choices, and communicates with consideration for the needs of his audience. He's got the timing, content, and volume down.

1.7 THE "ATTITUDE OF YOU"

A crucial aspect of corporate communication is the speaker's "you" mentality. The message's guiding premise must be the listener's or recipient's interest. After eventually forcing the hesitant Mr. X to hold back the two until they hear from head office, Mr. A notices this. Mr. X would not have Mr. A's primary justification for reclaiming the pair, which is to receive a response from head office. However, the other issue is that if Mr. X is not properly motivated by a receipt, the shoes can end up lost.

Due to his ability to communicate clearly from both his and the listener's points of view, Mr. A is able to successfully manipulate the entire scenario. In addition to promising to notify Mr. X over the phone, Mr. A uses audience-directed communication to persuade Mr. X to try contacting the showroom as well, just in case they don't get through.

Sincerity is a key component of Mr. A's communication style. The audience has to believe that the message is a sincere and trustworthy declaration of intent.

1.8 KEY ASPECTS OF BUSINESS COMMUNICATION

Mr. X is the main character in this case study. He exudes confidence and tenacious. He exudes the poise and ease of a well-dressed CEO of a large corporation. But in trying to make his argument, he loses his composure. He suddenly appears. Rather of attempting to persuade, he presses the matter.

Mr. X's attire, color scheme (olive green and bright orange), and choice of shoes and shorts (casual) all somewhat convey his attitude. In his arguments, he is just as casual. He leaps from one disagreement to the next to an alternative. The manufacturing flaw came first, followed by "seconds," and then his personal decision to avoid donning something unusual. The claim made by Mr. X that he was aware of it but did not give it any thought is not very strong. Additionally, Should he do so not to worry much, so why should he accept the opinions of others observations?

Mr. X approaches and behaves in a way that reflects his customer-centric mind set, believing that he is always the buyer and has the upper hand in negotiations. He is a Vice President in a global corporation. But he is the most lacking significant dimensions communication—the consistency, reason, and tone of convincing arguments. His talk with Mrs. X, who asserts to have informed him that "they won't take them back" demonstrates his belief in the possibility of coercion. We see that Mr. A makes different expressions than Mr. X that are aggressive in the nature. The difference is they made a claim that is clear from the language that those two speakers employed.

M. As a communicator, X has entirely fallen short.

1.9 USING APPROPRIATE LANGUAGE

A fundamental aspect of successful communication is the understanding and employing appropriate language for a certain objective. Additionally, as Language and communication are always intended to achieve specific goals. As a result, we must investigate the relationship between language and its intended application. One can use language to accomplish a combination of these goals, such as informing and persuading, in addition to creating, arguing, and persuading. Some students could believe that Mr. G had greater success as a communicator than others. He is transparent about his function and objective. He listens well, is forceful, and is courteous. Another powerful communication tool is listening. The same is true for Mr. G's situation—not communicating consciously is purposeful. In his capacity to assist in resolving the issue at the conflicting stage, he is strategic. He does not directly refute Mr. X's objection as a tactic. He doesn't start off by assuring Mr. X that he was mistaken and that the specific pair he purchased had no manufacturing flaws. Rather, he asks Mr. X gently, "You had not seen it at the time of buying them." And he included his "why?but only after allowing Mr. X to finish making his argument. That portrays Mr. G as a communicator who is unsure.

Mr. G is aware of the tactics of successful communication. He doesn't contradict himself. He doesn't try to persuade Mr. X that there wasn't a manufacturing or design flaw. Conversely, he emphasizes that the form was purposefully designed.

One should take heed of Mr. G's communication technique. He doesn't inform Mr. X up front that the duo wasn't "seconds." Rather, he answers in a detached manner. He tells Mr. X of the company's policy in a courteous manner. It is in bad circumstances that this impersonal communication works best.

Mr. G also employs the tactic of changing the subject of debate or conversation at a pivotal moment. Mr. X is obviously irritated and feeling powerless as he throws the two on the ground and tells Mr. G and Mr. A to do with them what they like. When Mr. X states that he does not have the receipt with him, Mr. G makes the psychological shift from the shoes to the receipt in this instance. Mr. G then abruptly leaves the situation, taking Mr. A with him. By doing this, he gives Mr. X the idea that he is accompanying Mr. A to talk about how they might support him. Mr. G allows Mr. A to come back with the last, definitive answer to the problem by putting a pause in their conversation.

There are some students who could think Mr. V is the best communicator. As the case's last adviser, he is succinct, has clear policy, is witty and decisive, assured and forceful, and, most importantly, is timely and unobtrusive. Depending on the customer's situation, he gives Mr. A particular instructions to follow.

The alternative viewpoint holds that Mr. V provides expert guidance. He should use direct language while speaking to a junior as a senior. Rather than offering Mr. A some straightforward counsel, his advise seems more like an order. The cliche "customer is king" is used by him to defend his treatment of affluent and poor clients differently. However, Mr. V's cunning is evident in the way he applies common sense to marketing strategy by using jargon, such as "a big and rich king to be saluted and the small and poor king to be simply shown the door."

Mrs. X, the last character in the case, speaks verbally briefly on the circumstances. However, we learn a great deal about her via her manner of communicating nonverbally. For instance, Mrs. X decides to remain away from the conversation scenario. Her being silent is purposeful. Because of it conveys that she was aware that attempting to retrieve the duo would be fruitless.

Her handbag and outfit convey her intention to come out with her spouse. Accompanied by him, she went shopping on her own. She seemed to have decided to spend some time window shopping when she decided to stay outside. However, given the circumstances, it appears like she withdrew on purpose to give Mr. X the opportunity to speak for himself. She didn't personally believe that the shoes could be returned. Mrs. X speaks in short, confident phrases. She is accurate. Compared to Mr. X, she talks and thinks more like Mr. A.

The fax that Mr. A sent to Mr. V demonstrates his capacity to communicate in writing because it includes written accounts of the incident's specifics, all of which were previously discussed orally. It provides a precise description of what happened. It is succinct and direct. It uses straightforward, conversational language. The statement has a particular raciness and a fluid flow of thoughts because of its brief sentences. Connectives like "in fact," "finally," and "but" are used to give his work cohesion and logic.

In his written message, Mr. A presents a factual account of the occurrence in a single, chronologically ordered paragraph. Mr. A is able to precisely portray the whole issue as it unfolded, as it progressed, and as the conclusion that was now being considered.

Every character in the case study exchanges information both orally and nonverbally. Spoken and written modes of communication are utilized in spoken interactions, converse, educate, defend, persuade, counsel, and teach. However, verbal source of every communication's power and significance is the individuality of the conveyer. The speaker's attire, gestures, body language, tone, clarity of approach, comprehension of the communication's subject matter, silence, and levity and assertiveness and aggression—all of which come together in order to form the meaning of the entire message delivered is determined by the communicator's personality in a certain context and relationship with the audience or recipient.

Additionally, the type of communication that is beneficial relies on a communicative personality. A communicator presents a personality with a certain center of focus and relationship to the person they are speaking to when they use certain words and word arrangements and avoid others. Like that Language self-dramatization is recognized as fashion. The speaker or author, selects his verbal and nonverbal communication style based on his personality.

Communication with the intention of establishing a certain focal point and connection with the audience. In different statements, the full action of Communication is a sign of one's attitude, worries, and state of mind toward both the issue and himself/her audience.

1.10 7 C'S OF COMMUNICATION

Effective communication is essential for success in the corporate sector. Both written and spoken communication contribute to achieving excellence in communication. Understanding the seven C's of communication is crucial for successfully conveying key messages, which in turn enhances employee engagement and productivity. The 7Cs of communication are:

1) Clarity

2) Correctness

3) Conciseness

4) Courtesy

5) Concreteness

6) Consideration

7) Completeness

We'll talk about each of them individually:

1) Clarity

Rather than attempting to send too many messages at once, this indicates that a single message has been conveyed. Utilizing clear and accurate services is required for this.

The qualities of clarity are as follows:

- Excellent comprehension

- Precision of concepts and ideas
- Use of clear, acceptable, and simple language

2) Correctness:

To effectively convey information, it is crucial to use proper terminology, grammar, and facts. The characteristics of accuracy are:

- Accurate, precise, and timely communication
- Enhancement of self-assurance
- Greater influence on the audience

3) Conciseness:

This refers to speaking in a way that requires the fewest possible words. It possesses the following qualities:

- Saves time
- Prevents overuse of superfluous words
- Brief and concise
- Clear and easy to understand
- Non-repetitive

4) Courtesy:

This is one of the most crucial Cs of communication because it fosters goodwill by treating the other person with respect and acting sensibly. It possesses the following qualities:

- Taking into account the emotions of the audience

☐ Sincere and focused
☐ Objective

5) Concreteness:

This refers to something that is precise, significant, and obvious, staying clear of uncertainty and avoiding ambiguity and dual meanings. It has the following features:

- Backs up statements with numbers and facts
- Accurate and detailed
- Prevents misunderstandings

6) Consideration:

This suggests that the viewpoints, culture, mindset, values, and other aspects of the audience are taken into account. It has the following characteristics:

- Focuses on the "you" approach
- Caring
- Optimistic

7) Completeness:

Completeness is the last C in communication. It implies that any connection, whether private or professional, needs to be comprehensive. It ought to present all the information and details needed to convey the following features:

- Enhances the standing of the company
- Cost saving
- Eliminates obstacles caused by imprecise information
- Facilitates improved decision-making

Understanding the seven Cs of communication makes it evident that communication is one of the most fundamental skills that need to be practiced.

Activity 3

For each of the 7 C's of successful communication, write an example.

7C's of Communication	Example
Clarity	
Correctness	
Conciseness	
Courtesy	
Concreteness	
Consideration	
Completeness	

1.11 SUMMARY

We have covered the concept, history, and specific function of communication in this unit. The way we communicate has changed over time, greatly impacted by technology in the modern era, beginning with symbols. Our attitudes and beliefs significantly affect how we interact. Business communication and general communication are not the same. They differ in format, category, extent, presentation, goals, nature, and feedback. Through the case study, we have explored the aspects of communication and the use of appropriate language. We have also learned the seven Cs of communication: clarity, correctness, conciseness, courtesy, concreteness, consideration, and completeness. This aids in our understanding of the appropriate communication style for each situation.

1.12 KEY TERMS

- Transmitting ideas, thoughts, or information from one person to another is called **Communication**.
- Communication pertaining to corporate operations is referred to as **"Business Communication."**
- **Concreteness** is the quality of communication in which a message should be precise and unambiguous.
- **Courtesy** is the act of acting with decency and civility toward other people.

1.13 QUESTIONS FOR SELF-ASSESSMENT

1. Talk about the function of business communication in corporate settings.

2. Examine the "you" attitude as a crucial component of professional communication.

3. "A communication is successful only if its goal is achieved." Describe.

4. Talk about the idea that listening is a crucial part of communication.

5. Describe the various verbal and nonverbal ways that people communicate in business environment.

Unit 2

THE COMMUNICATION PROCESS

OBJECTIVES

After completing this unit, you should be capable of:

- Gain an understanding of the process of two-way communication
- Identify barriers to communication
- Learn how to overcome obstacles in communication

STRUCTURE

2.1 Introduction

2.2 The Linear Concept of Communication

2.3 The Shannon-Weaver Model of Communication

2.4 The Process of Two-Way Communication

2.5 Barriers to Communication

2.6 Intrapersonal Barriers

2.7 Interpersonal Barriers

2.8 The Organizational Barriers

2.9 Case Study

2.10 Summary

2.11 Key Terms

2.12 Questions of Self-Assessment

2.1 INTRODUCTION

One of the most fundamental aspects of every person or organization is their ability to communicate. An efficient method of communication exists. Consequently, in order to prevent the typical blunders that occur during communication, it is critical that we comprehend the process of human communication. Various models of communication are covered in this course to help comprehend the process. Both one-way and two-way communication are possible. We will explore many models that might assist us in comprehending the flow of communication. In addition to these models, we will also discuss the obstacles to communication.

2.2 THE LINEAR CONCEPT OF COMMUNICATION

When first starting a conversation, it's common to ask these five basic questions:

1. Who says it?
2. What is said?
3. Where is it said?
4. Who is being addressed?
5. What is the impact of what is said?

Data transfer is defined as the process by which one party transfers data to another party. From a linear perspective, a listener receives the message and complies with the instructions or requests made by the sender. The goal of communication is to exert influence over the person receiving the message, assuming that the reception of the message is unaltered.

2.3: SHANNON-WEAVER COMMUNICATION MODEL

Presented by C.E. Shannon and W. Weaver, the Shannon-Weaver communication model acknowledges that messages may undergo changes or obstacles during the process of transmission. The model is constructed based on a mathematical or automated understanding of the message conveying process, addressing the core issue that transmitted and received messages may not be identical. In the latter half of 1949, the Shannon model was introduced as an explanation of communication grounded in mathematics, developed in collaboration with Weaver. Weaver initially proposed the use of feedback to mitigate background noise, contrasting with the Shannon-Weaver model's perspective, which regarded feedback as an independent act of communication rather than essential to the process.

The Shannon-Weaver model, operates on the premise that communication can only occur once a message has been received, ideally without distortion. However, this notion represents an idealized concept of communication. In reality, various filters influence how the sender's and receiver's thoughts are conveyed through communication. The feedback loop in the model helps to close the communication loop and rectify any distortions.

Source of Information

The information source is the initial step in the communication process. At this stage, the sender possesses raw data that has not yet been processed. The intention is to convert this information into a message that can be shared. Every communication process originates from an information source or "source," from which messages are transmitted.

Encoding

Symbols, whether spoken or written, are carefully considered by the sender before the message is composed. This process is called encoding.

Channel of Transmission

Any appropriate means of communication, whether spoken, written, electronic, coded, or through a signaling system, can be described as a channel.

Decoding

Decoding involves receiving, understanding, and interpreting the message. The receiver engages in this process to perceive the message accurately.

Acting

When the recipient takes the desired action based on the meaning of an interpreted message, the Communication process is complete.

Because of this, we can see that communication is cyclical, uniting the sender and the receiver as one. The capacity to effectively communicate is seen as crucial for modern managers due to the unifying nature of the process and the function it plays.

Noise

The transmission of messages from the sender to the receiver might be disrupted or distorted by noise if this mechanism is not properly protected.

Some theorists of communication define "noise" as external disruptions to the physical setting of a communication session, such as low-quality audio, dropped calls, illegible printed materials, or other similar issues.

Filters

Subjective factors, such the attitudes of the sender and the recipient, cause distortion in communication, and filters are to blame for this. These pertain to the mind/intellect. Among these are one's attitude, beliefs, experiences, self-awareness, and capacity for rational thought. The receiver's experience, knowledge, and feelings serve as filters through which the sender's communication passes, increasing the likelihood of misunderstandings and other problems.

2.4 THE TWO-WAY PROCESS OF COMMUNICATION

Subsequent theories of communication have expanded it to include both parties. To round out the communication cycle, the receiver also acts as the sender of feedback to the transmitter. The roles of the sender and the receiver are reversible and reciprocal, similar to telemarketing or communication in call centres.

The dual method is more contemporary, viewing communication primarily as a two-way street where messages are both sent and received. Often, the same person acts as both the sender and the recipient, blurring the line between the two roles.

In contrast to the previous linear viewpoint, where the sender held ultimate authority over the message's meaning, the two-way concept considers the recipient as an integral part of the message creation and understanding process. The recipient's application of their own values, thoughts, and emotions to the message becomes paramount. Over time, as individuals share experiences and develop shared beliefs and values within their workplace or community, they tend to perceive things through a shared lens. Another term for two-way communication is transactional communication. Additionally, in Unit 6, we will delve deeper into the transactional model.

2.5 BARRIERS TO COMMUNICATION

Understanding the nature of the obstacles in a communication process is essential for overcoming or avoiding them. A barrier acts like a sieve, letting just a fraction of the message through while blocking the desired response. If you want to communicate well in the workplace, no matter what your role is, you need to know how barriers function, why they cause misunderstandings, and how to lessen their impact. Even with the best of intentions, miscommunication could occur, leading to statements like "I intended to say this but didn't!" or "I meant to say that but didn't!"

There are several types of communication barriers, such as:

- Interpersonal
- Intrapersonal
- Organisational

2.6. INTRAPERSONAL BARRIERS

Each person is special in his own way due to differences in perspective, background, upbringing, culture, and personality. Because our thoughts vary, we interpret the same facts differently. These differences are the result of inherent or intrapersonal barriers. Let's look at all the typical reasons that lead to these barriers.

- Wrong assumption
- Varied Perception
- Different Background
- Wrong Inference
- Blocked Categories
- Categorical Thinking

Wrong Assumptions

Assumptions are a common source of communication breakdowns; for instance, if a doctor tells a patient to take medicine only in an emergency (i.e., "SOS") without checking with the patient to see if they know what the phrase means, the doctor has created a barrier to effective communication because he or she has assumed too much about the patient's level of knowledge.

Whether one party is lacking in information about the other's background or has long-held misconceptions, it's easy to fall into the trap of making assumptions. To improve your communication abilities, try putting yourself in the other person's shoes. This will help you avoid making assumptions about their knowledge or abilities. No one is new to the tale of the six blind men and an elephant. The elephant came to symbolize various things to different men: a fan, a rope, a snake, a sword, wall, tree. All the blind men were correct; the area of the elephant's body that each man felt was comparable to the things they had mentioned. This is how different people have diverse perspectives on the same thing.

Just as various people in an organization may have different interpretations of the same facts, the key to overcoming this obstacle is to gain some distance and look at the problem from a new angle.

Varied Perceptions

Because of variations in upbringing, language, culture, environment, and financial status, no two people's backgrounds are identical. Consequently, our backgrounds significantly impact our interpretation of any given message.

In order to have better communication skills, it's important to know who you're talking to and what they're about. With this knowledge, you can build your message more appropriately. Empathy, or identifying with another person, is the key to overcoming this barrier. Try to figure out what the listener might not understand because our backgrounds are different. Use the language the receiver understands to avoid ambiguity and reduce multiple   meanings.

Wrong Inferences

Consider the following scenario: you're back from a business trip and find out that two of your co-workers are missing. They don't show up for a few days. Since there's a recession going on, you assume that they've been promoted and moved to another department. This is an example of fact-inference confusion, which occurs when you fail to differentiate between what actually exists and what you assumed to exist.

It is vital that professionals analyse materials, solve issues, and develop procedures using facts supporting inferences since, being more dramatic than facts, inferences could lead to the spread of rumours and gossips.

Blocked Categories

When we encounter information that runs counter to our own views, habits, or attitudes, or that seems unfavourable to us, our natural inclination is to react negatively or even reject it. The three most prevalent negative responses to unwelcome information are distortion, avoidance, and rejection.

People who are resistant or closed-minded find it difficult to adapt to the fast-paced changes occurring in communication and other technologies; rather than seizing the opportunities presented by these innovations, which speed up the communication process, they fight and criticize them.

On the flip side, people who are very dogmatic about their views may have trouble expressing themselves clearly; for instance, one of your classmates might think that only students majoring in science can think critically; another might think that young executives are more effective than older executives; these people are called "blocked" because they can't stand to hear anything that contradicts their beliefs.

Categorical Thinking

This kind of thinking can be a major obstacle, leading to a barrier to communication, because people who think they know everything about a subject will not accept any further knowledge about this subject.

A hint to recognizing this barrier in ourselves and others is the use of words like "all," "always," "everybody," "everything," and their opposites, such as "none," "never," "nobody," and "nothing." If a message contains too many of these words, the communication is likely to get distorted. To avoid this, replace them with phrases like "in most situations" or "most likely." To label your viewpoints, use terms like "it appears to me" or "the evidence shows." If your data is sufficient, it is preferable to admit that you are uninformed of the remaining facts rather than to be vague.

2.7 INTERPERSONAL BARRIERS

Individual attitudes and habits are the root cause of intrapersonal barriers, whereas limited communication abilities of the coder or decoder, or both, are the root cause of interpersonal barriers. Disruptions to the communication route or medium can also cause these barriers to emerge. When two people are communicating, the characteristics that distinguish them as individuals can be the source of a communication gap.

While it's unrealistic to expect businesspeople to magically transform their personalities, it is possible to gain insight into the ways in which these disparities manifest as communication hurdles. Few words to choose from discord between spoken and non-spoken communication.

- Limited Vocabulary
- Incompatibility of verbal and non-verbal message
- Emotional outburst
- Communicational selectivity
- Poor listening skills
- Noise in the channel

Limited Vocabulary

One of the biggest obstacles to effective communication is a limited vocabulary. When we are giving a speech, stumbling over words can reflect poorly on the speaker and their message influence the audience. Conversely, a big and diverse vocabulary can assist us in creating a favourable impression on our listeners.

Incompatibility of verbal and non-verbal message

Mixed signals conveyed via speech and body language not only should one make an effort to read the nonverbal clues of others, but one should also be aware of their own body language, as nonverbal signals give a more nuanced understanding of the information that a sender is trying to convey.

One of the most significant non-verbal clues is one's physical appearance, thus making judgments based on these assumptions can also lead to serious communication hurdles. In order to make a good first impression, one might adhere to specific rules for improving their physical appearance, such as:

- Put on the correct attire for the occasion.
- Retire your garments neat and clean.
- Select an appropriate hairstyle.
- Keep your shoes clean and shiny.

Emotional Outburst

Most of the time, when people's emotions are moderately high, it makes communication easier. When people's emotions are extremely high, though, it can be a barrier to communication. Extreme anger, for instance, can make it hard to have a reasonable discussion because of the emotionally charged atmosphere it creates. Prejudice, stereotyping, and boredom are other factors that make it hard to have effective communication. Positive emotions, like excitement and happiness, can also interfere with communication, but not nearly as much as negative feelings.

There are times when people react negatively, and depending on the person and the situation, this negative reaction can be either hostile or defensive. Both reactions happen when the person receiving the message perceives a threat; hostileness is a counter-attack, and defensiveness is resistance to the threat. Emotions are an essential part of being human, whether in a professional or personal setting. Emotions can help create an environment that is highly conducive to good communication by honing self-awareness, intention, and empathy.

Keeping one's cool in any conversation is crucial. Learning to see things from other people's points of view may help one become more objective and logical, which in turn can help one avoid becoming defensive or hostile.

Communication Selectivity

A communication barrier known as "communication selectivity" occurs when the receiver focuses on just a subset of the message due to a narrow interest in that subset.

Method of Expression- Communication that may be helpful to the recipient; in this instance, the sender is not at fault; rather, it is the recipient who causes a disruption in the transmission. Consider a scenario where the chief executive officer (CEO) of a company calls a meeting of all the senior executives from different departments, such as production, marketing, finance, and human resources (HR). During the meeting, the CEO covers a lot of ground, but he or she may not be able to convey the full meaning of what has been said. For example, when a boss is talking to an employee but keeps moving the papers around on their desk instead of making eye contact, it shows that they are only paying half attention to what the employee is saying. This behavior can harm the boss-subordinate relationship and undermine the message they are trying to convey.

Cultural Variations

One of the most common interpersonal factors that lead to

communication breakdowns is the fact that people from different cultural backgrounds and language backgrounds have different perspectives on how to work together effectively. This is especially true in today's globalized business world, where companies are aiming to outperform their domestic and international competitors. Many multinational corporations have gone global, forming international partnerships, collaborations, and affiliations. As a result, these companies' management and employees must be well-versed in the laws, customs, and business practices of the countries in which they operate, all while interacting with their multinational workforce. To succeed in this kind of environment, it is necessary to learn how to communicate effectively across cultural and linguistic boundaries.

Poor listening skills

Misunderstandings and disputes can be avoided if individuals pay close attention to the message. The different distractions that hinder listening include emotional disturbances, indifferences, aggression, and wandering attention. It is important to remember that listening and hearing are different. Hearing is a passive activity, while listening involves deliberate attention and correct decoding of the speaker's information.

Some people are so preoccupied with their own problems that they forget to listen. For example, when a boss is talking to an employee, but keeps moving the papers around on his desk instead of looking them in the eyes, it shows that he or she is paying half attention to what the employee is saying, which is bad for the boss-subordinate relationship and the message they are trying to convey.

Noise in the Channel

Unwanted signals that interfere with communication are called noise. Noise can be audible, but it can also be visual, audio-visual, textual, physical, or psychological. All of these forms of noise transmit extra information that might subtract from the message and annoy the person receiving it.

The term "technical noise" can describe a variety of different types of background noise, including but not limited to: the roar of machinery, the thump-thump of a stereo system, and any number of other sounds that drown out human speech, such as a tardy attendee or someone who arrives late to a meeting and diverts everyone's focus away from the presenters.

2.8 ORGANIZATIONAL BARRIERS

Even inside organizations, there are communication barriers; every business, no matter how big or little, has its own communication methods and must adapt to its particular communication environment.

Feedback is not guaranteed in large organizations with a downward flow of communication. Organizations with a flat structure typically have a tightly knit communication network. Regardless of size, all organizations have communication policies that outline the protocol to be followed. The issue with communication barriers typically arises from the structure and complexity of this protocol.

Many big companies have realized that communication is hindered by strict hierarchical structures. This is because the communication flow in such systems has many transfer points, which can lead to message distortion, delay, or loss. To circumvent these problems, it is preferable to have sender-receiver contact or to transmit the message with minimum transfer stations.

Organizational Barriers mostly include:

- Too many transfer stations
- Fear of superior
- Negative Tendency
- Use of inappropriate media
- Information overload

Too many transfer stations

The likelihood of misunderstanding increases as the number of links in a communication chain increases. For example, let's say your professor asks you to relay a message to X. Due to some inconvenience or sheer laziness, you ask your friend Y to do it. Now there are four people involved in this communication channel. What happens is that the message gets distorted because the number of transfer stations increases.

Professor: I was hoping that X and I might meet today to go over the Business Communication project, but I'll be out of the office tomorrow, so I'd rather have X come in on Friday.

You should ask X to meet with the professor tomorrow to discuss the work because the professor is leaving on a trip today, and Y's professor is also leaving today.

Y to X: Hey X, the professor isn't accessible tomorrow, so you better meet with him now.

Having too many transfer stations is always an obstacle to effective communication and should be avoided. While they do serve a purpose, having too many is counter-productive. This is an example of how messages get distorted in large organizations with several layers of communication channels. Each level of distorting the message can be caused by poor listening or lack of concentration, among other things. Some employees may filter out parts of the message they consider unimportant.

Fear of Superior

In highly structured organizations, subordinates are often afraid to speak their minds for fear of reprimand or embarrassment from their superiors. As a result, employees may either avoid communicating with their bosses altogether or give their bosses every piece of information they possess, leading to lengthy reports that include important details mixed in with irrelevant details. This kind of disorganized communication causes a lot of time to be wasted.

Negative Tendencies

While some groups are formed to accomplish specific tasks, such as finishing a specific project, other smaller groups are formed for social, recreational, or community purposes. These groups, whether formal or informal, typically include people who share similar values, beliefs, behavior, attitudes, and opinions. However, communication can become strained when there is conflict between group members and those who are not part of the group. An example of an insider-outsider equation that can lead to negative tendencies in an organization is when non-student members of a school's sports club try to block the distribution of additional funds for sports equipment, which can annoy the student members of the club.

Use of Inappropriate Media

Phone calls, emails, online presentations, teleconferences, and video conferences are all viable options for various types of communication, but before settling on one, it's important to weigh the pros, cons, and possible obstacles.

- Time
- Type of message
- Cost
- Intended Audience

As an example, sensitive information should not be communicated over the phone but rather in person or through a private chat messenger if the recipient is in a different office. Written letters are preferable for information that needs to be saved and retrieved later on because they are permanent. To ensure effective communication, it is common to use a combination of mediums, such as email followed by a phone call.

Information Overload

One of the biggest problems that companies are facing now is the inefficiency that comes from having to manually process massive amounts of data. This is called information overload, and it usually leads to people becoming tired, uninterested, and bored. When this happens, further communication breaks down, and important and crucial information gets lost among all the irrelevant data. Therefore, quality of information is far more important than quantity.

Screening information is essential for reducing information overload in an organization. Messages should be sent to those individuals most likely to benefit from them. Emphasizing important elements while removing unnecessary ones is key.

2.9 THE CASE STUDY

Now, to further understand the idea of communication failure, let's look at a case study.

Communication Failure

Mr. and Mrs. S went to Max Apparel to buy a pullover. Mr. S didn't read the price tag, so he asked the cashier for the price. The clerk told him it was 950/-. While he was paying, Mrs. S returned to the store to join her husband. She was happy that he had chosen a nice white pullover. She pointed out that the item was 25% off, and the clerk nodded in agreement. Mr. S was ecstatic to hear that. "It means the price of this pullover is 712/-. That's fantastic," he exclaimed.

He chose to purchase an additional green pullover. Quickly after, he returned with the second set of pullovers and requested that they be packaged. To his surprise, when asked how much he needed to pay, he discovered that it was 1900/- instead of 1424/-.

The decreased price of ₹950/-, which the counter worker had mentioned, was hard for Mr. S to accept, especially because the original price on the tag was ₹1266/-.

Activity 1

a) Name the three sources from which Mr. S obtained his knowledge

....

\ ....

....

....

....

b) Talk about the biggest obstacle here with example.

....
....
....
....
....

c) How could Mr. S have prevented the miscommunication?

....

....

....

....

....

d) Who is responsible for the breakdown in communication and why?

....
....
....
....

2.10 SUMMARY

We have learned about both one-way and two-way communication in this unit. We have also gained an understanding of human communication and its processes, which will help us avoid common mistakes when communicating. This unit focuses on the linear concept of communication, which is a one-way process in which the sender transmits the send a 34-character message to another model without receiving any kind of response.

This unit began with an overview of the Shannon-Weaver Model, which revealed that messages can be blocked during communication and led to the introduction of feedback. It then moved on to cover the two-way process of communication, barriers to communication (intrapersonal, interpersonal, and organizational), and finally, a case study that covered all the aspects of the process.

2.11 KEY TERMS

The term **"Feedback"** refers to the reaction that a message's recipient provides to its sender.

Intrapersonal Barriers: These are the parts of a person's character that get in the way of good communication.

Factors outside of an individual's control that could impede their ability to communicate effectively are known as **interpersonal barriers**.

Disruption to the free flow of information among an organization's workers is an example of an **organizational barrier**.

2.12 QUESTIONS FOR PERSONAL EVALUATION

1) Discuss that 'The Two-Way Model of Communication' and 'The Shannon-Weaver Model' are not the Same.

2) Describe one or more intrapersonal obstacles to communication.

3) Give instances to illustrate the difference between interpersonal and intrapersonal communication difficulties.

4) Describe the most significant obstacles to communication at your workplace.

5) Using examples, define the following concepts as they pertain to obstacles in communication:

- Emotional Outburst
- Cultural differences
- 'Know-it-all'
- attitude

UNIT 3

TYPES OF COMMUNICATION

OBJECTIVES

After studying this unit you will be able to:

- Understand the difference between verbal and non-verbal communication
- Explain different types of verbal communication;
- Understand the different types of non-verbal communication and theirrole in our life.

STRUCTURE

3.1 Introduction

3.2 Verbal Communication

3.3 Types of Verbal Communication

3.4 Non-Verbal Communication

3.5 Types of Non-verbal Communication

3.6 Summary

3.7 Keywords

3.8 Self-Assessment Questions

3.9 References and Further Readings

DR. RUCHI TANDON &
DR. LALIT KR. YADAV

3.1 INTRODUCTION

"A blow with a word strikes deeper than a fistfight," reportedly remarked Robert Burton impact using an armament. Consequently, you must be sure to choose your words carefully and wisely, as it decides how well our conversation goes on both an individual and an organizational level. The realms of our private and public lives glide down the paths of dialogue. Personal and professional success accrue more to those who are skilled communicators than to those who are not, especially when communicating with someone whose skill level is average or below average.

When providing advice, counseling, coaching, or mentorship, it is crucial to communicate effectively. This involves delegating responsibilities, discussing potential health risks, preparing marketing materials, and including marketing strategies in the plan. The bulk of spoken communication involves nonverbal cues such as posture, angle, velocity, and direction, as well as facial expressions. According to Overton, almost half of the message sent by the communicator is conveyed through means other than speech. He also reports that only 7% of a message's meaning is conveyed through the actual words spoken, while 38% of the message's impact relies on how it is expressed. Both verbal and nonverbal communication play essential roles in everyday discourse, whether in informal conversations or professional settings. This section will cover the specifics of various forms of communication to distinguish between them and appreciate their significance.

3.2 VERBAL COMMUNICATION

In both one's personal and professional lives, verbal communication encompasses all interactions through speech, listening, and writing. Simply said, verbal communication is the process by which two or more individuals establish contact with one another via the use of spoken or written language. Whether spoken or written, the message travels from its originator to its recipient. Therefore, verbal communication encompasses both written and spoken forms of expression. Messages can go from sender to receiver in a one-way communication, with no feedback loop in between. On the other hand, in a two-way communication, the exchange takes place between two parties, with the sender sending a message and the recipient responding. They collaborate harmoniously toward a same objective, share knowledge, and dispel confusion.

3.3 TYPES OF VERBAL COMMUNICATION

Basically verbal communication can be classified into two categories and they are -

- Oral communication
- Written communication

Oral communication is something where we speak with someone through words whereas written communication includes the words which are in a written form. Let us now discuss these types of communication.

Oral Communication

In both our personal and professional lives, this is by far the most popular and prevalent form of communication. Establishing communication through spoken words is what oral communication entails, as previously mentioned. Communication can be official, casual, one-way, or two-way. Meeting in person, talking on the phone, or communicating via video conferencing are all viable options. Put simply, it entails a communicator (the one delivering the message) and an audience (the one receiving it), either one or numerous listeners. The situation dictates whether the speaker and listener engage in one-way or two-way communication.

Formal and informal modes of oral communication coexist. Conversations between friends, relatives, and coworkers on subjects unrelated to work or other formal settings provide examples of informal oral communication. Relationships between individuals constitute the basis of informal oral communication, which is characterized by its casual tone. Because of its informal character, it often takes place outside of the formal structures of universities, companies, and schools.

Conversely, organizational hierarchies and the line of command govern official spoken communication, which does not include the casual interchange of information. Following this, management has instituted stringent rules confined by time and structure to regulate the flow of information.

There are contexts in which the use of formal, spoken language is religiously observed. Communication such as depositions, speeches, lectures, viva voce, oral evaluations, lecturing, classroom discussions, and corporate meetings. This meeting is between the school's administration and the faculty or staff, or between the management team and the employees. The notification of a plane, train, bus, etc., scheduled departure or arrival is one example of an instance where the message has to be transmitted rapidly. Speaking in an official capacity and using proper grammar and punctuation make formal oral communication more trustworthy.

Oral communication that is not formal. Most people say things in a more informal tone, thus there aren't as many formal channels of authority to rely on when communicating. In informal environments, information flows freely, unlike in formal settings where it follows predetermined channels.

Written Communication

Written communication involves conveying information through written language. The sender transmits their message using written text in this form of communication. It includes various forms such as letters, instructions, reports, emails, manuals, publications, and guides. Written communication is highly effective because it provides documentation that can be saved for future reference or used as a permanent record. Unlike spoken language, written expression tends to be more formal and lacks the natural flexibility of verbal communication.

Because it includes documentation that can be saved or become a permanent record for future use, written communication is a very effective kind of communication. Unlike spoken language, written expression is largely formal and lacks natural flexibility.

Professionals rely on written documents since they can be used as proof in legal situations. Formal language is typically employed in this type of communication. We avoid using abbreviations or jargon and instead use whole sentences and words. Written conversing is also highly favoured in less formal contexts. Written communication is essential in today's era of social media and multimedia message.

Every form of written communication has its advantages and disadvantages. Compared to spoken language, written communication is generally slower, as information dissemination through text involves an anticipation period during which the recipient cannot access the communication. This can be particularly cumbersome, especially in official discourse regulated by managerial and bureaucratic hierarchies within organizational structures.

Additionally, it dependents upon the individual's level of literacy. Conversely, the ability to read and write is not necessary for the transmission of information by spoken word. We begin speaking far more frequently as infants and have the innate capacity to learn new languages.

The ability to express oneself in writing is a lifelong skill. The mastery of this mode of expression requires extensive training over many years. Even before learning to write, a young child can pick up a language simply by seeing and copying others around them. It is widely acknowledged that language acquisition occurs in a social context and is innate to humans. Literacy is thus not a prerequisite for taking part in oral communication. The process is quicker and more organic. Contrarily, written communication is slower and relies on a person's reading level. Both oral and written communication skills are vital for success in our personal and professional lives, so it's important to master both.

Activity 1

Make a list of the formal and informal verbal communication mediums you use in your everyday life. Explain which medium of verbal communication isused more frequently and why?

....

....

....

....

3.4 NON-VERBAL COMMUNICATION

Words, whether spoken or written, are not necessary for any kind of communication. The speaker in this type of communication typically does not use words but rather non-verbal clues to convey meaning. According to the opinions of many experts, it makes up over half of the communication process, making it an integral aspect of the process. Visual or auditory cues can constitute non-verbal communication. Some examples of visual non-verbal cues include signs, symbols, gestures, body language, facial expressions, eye contact, and outward appearance. One kind of auditory nonverbal communication is a platoon of soldiers marching in time with a drum beat, which they achieve by following a pattern of varying lengths and notes. Another example could be the unique manner in which a school bell governs the school's schedule.

 Many parts of our lives are controlled by non-verbal communication. Signs and symbols are always there, interacting with us. Typically, these discussions only go one way. The traffic lights, for instance, are in constant communication with a huge number of commuters; they direct their actions to ensure a smooth flow of traffic and prevent an otherwise chaotic scenario.

For one-way communication, there are a lot of symbols that work. Using seemingly little images, like a motorcycle or a telephone, they convey crucial information to us.

The above notice informs commuters that there is a road restriction that prohibits doing a U-turn. People who aren't good readers can nonetheless understand and follow the most important traffic laws thanks to these non-verbal signs and symbols. Consider the case of a non-English speaking country that receives an international driver's license from an English speaking nation. The individual will be able to communicate with the road using these symbols and signs. While men and women use different terms to describe the same thing, making use of gender-specific symbols makes utilizing public restrooms much easier.

Because the same signs and symbols can be used anywhere, non-verbal communication is a worldwide type of communication that is not limited by language limitations. The illiterate can be included in all main activities with the help of these signs and symbols. For instance, a symbol is used by each political party to identify a candidate, which helps voters who are illiterate. Choosing the ideal candidate from among selecting an option from a vast pool of individuals running for office in a certain election. It addresses two distinct viewpoints. First, it expedites the process and aids the illiterate in choosing a candidate. Secondly, voting will be faster if voters who are literate simply look at the symbols to indicate which candidate they support, rather than reading the names.

Imagine a cricket or football match now. There are just too many people at these games for there to be any way to communicate with them while still delivering the story of the sport. To let everyone know when a player is out or has scored a boundary, a cricket umpire uses hand gestures. A football referee communicates with the audience using flags, colored cards, and other gestures. All people around the world recognize and adhere to these set movements and symbols. Regardless of a spectator's language or cultural background, these signs, gestures, and symbols allow them to follow the action on the field during a football match. Now we have these straight forward two-way dialogue on top of failing to demand verbal expression (verbal or otherwise). Therefore, non-verbal communication plays a significant role in our daily lives, particularly in situations where the communication is one-sided and aimed at a broad group of people. Along with verbal communication, non-verbal cues are useful in other contexts where language is required.

Take a look at table 1 for the benefits and problems with non-verbal communication.

Table 1: Advantages and disadvantages of non-verbal communication

S. No	Advantages	Disadvantages
1.	It is very useful for one way communication when a person or a large group of people needs to understand a simple message quickly.	It can only be a one-way communication in most cases.
2.	It is easy to understand and people almost act instinctively on specific signs, symbols etc.	The meaning of the message is fixed and limited.
3.	Literacy of a language is not essential in comprehending nonverbal signs and symbols.	People need to learn the meaning of a particular sign. Traffic signs interpreted incorrectly may result in an accident.
4.	A very large data set can be presented through graphs, charts etc.	Making and interpreting these graphs, charts etc. require professional training. It can be time consuming and expensive. It also requires literacy skills.

5.	Most of these signs and symbols are universal and are not governed by language boundaries.	Installing and maintaining these signs, symbols for mass consumption has its recurring cost and can be a burden on finances. Improper signs, boards, hoardings can either incorrectly guide someone or may divert the attention of the drivers resulting in an accident.
6.	It facilitates the ease of communication.	These signs may be interpreted incorrectly sometimes and may result in miscommunication

Activity 2

Examine the following instances and provide at least three case studies involving non-verbal communication in front of a large group of people.

For instance, ensuring that children aged 0-5 receive a vaccine. Two days in October 2021 have been set aside for the polio vaccination campaign.

....

....

....

....

....

3.5 TYPES OF NON-VERBAL COMMUNICATION

Now, let's discuss the various forms of non-verbal communication. Classifying non-verbal means of communication can be quite challenging because there are many different items that fall within the realm of non-verbal interaction. Generally, it can be classified as:

kinesics (Body language, emotional state, gaze nonverbal communication, prose), and Interactions between space and time, Symbols of nonverbal communication, such as silence, haptics, and paralanguage.

Kinesics

As a field of research, kinesics focuses on how the body communicates through its physical movements. Simply put, nonverbal communication is the art of conveying meaning through the use of nonverbal cues such as body language, facial expressions, eye contact, and the like. For instance, when someone nods their head, it means they are accepting or rejecting. Some of the physical motions we do while talking are deliberate, while others are unconscious. The conscious movements in conjunction with the significance of unconscious gestures in communicating our message cannot be overstated. We may learn about kinesics by examining the following parameters for the better, since these metrics are crucial in the corporate sphere.

Physical Appearance:

Although it has little to do with how the body moves, our first impression is often based on how we seem. Before we even think about talking to someone, it is a need. First impressions are often based on how we look. Everything from our hairdo to the accessories we wear—whether it's a watch, pen, or perfume—

contributes to our physical look. Clothes and other everyday objects, such as a pen or watch, now serve more as means of self-expression. Cultured and educated people tend to dress more formally and accessorize appropriately than others who only dress to meet their basic necessities or who don't bother to keep their hair neat.

Posture:

The second component is our posture, which is essentially our outward appearance. The way we move about while talking, standing, walking, sitting, and holding ourselves is all part of body language. As a component of communication, it changes depending on the context in which we are conveying our messages. It says a lot about who we are as individuals, so it's crucial. A lack of self-assurance or competence could be conveyed by an anxious posture. Additionally, it clarifies how much expertise we possess as speakers of a specific language. A self-assured public speaker knows their stuff and can captivate listeners with their enthusiasm and knowledge. Keeping our hands and legs still, not twitching, and not fidgeting with our phones or pens is important for projecting an image of self-assurance.

Gestures:

Hand, head, and facial movements are all part of the language we use. The efficacy of the communication could be compromised if the amount of gestures is excessive or insufficient. Nodding our head to indicate agreement or disagreement is a great way to enhance what we say verbally, but it may also render our words useless if we use it wrong. Keep your hand movements moderate and not clumsy. Using the motions effectively takes some practice and planning.

Facial Expressions :

Facial Expressions convey the speaker's intent and are thus an essential aspect of communication. It is crucial for the messenger to amplify his or her words with suitable facial expressions because we may deduce the speaker's goal just by observing their faces. A motivational speaker, for instance, should maintain an upbeat demeanor and project the enthusiasm they wish to inspire their listeners. An upbeat and inspiring message will be undermined by a glum or unhappy look.

 Make direct eye contact with the people in the room; this will alter the impact your message has on them. We convey a lot of information with our eyes. Looking someone in the eyes while you speak can make all the difference in the world.

Eye Contact

A brief overview of discourse more impactful. However, making no direct eye contact Communication could make the listeners uninterested and give the impression that the speaker lacks confidence. Another possibility is that the listeners would think the speaker is clueless when it comes to the topic at hand. You must remember to make the right kind of eye contact. The presenter must not to fixate on the ear, on the other hand, aim to make direct eye contact in order to confirm that "s/he is" determined to communicate the message to the audience. Making and keeping eye contact reassures the audience of your attentiveness, self-assurance, and readiness to the person delivering the speech to initiate dialogue along with the person who is listening.

However, looking down or away from the speaker indicates that they are nervous, shy, or uninterested in what they are saying.

Activity 3

Gather 10 or more images of people from media, including magazines perhaps even wide web. These images should convey a range of emotions through their faces and actions.

Sign Language

One of the most advanced forms of non-verbal communication is sign language. The language is based on signs and symbols that are audible, visible, and hybrid. As we have previously established, the majority of the world's non-verbal communicators use sign language. There are signs and symbols that are commonly used and recognized all over the world. But there are signals and symbols that are culturally particular, and people from various cultures may interpret them differently. In Western culture, a thumbs-up is a sign of agreement or encouragement; however, on the Indian subcontinent, it is a symbol of rejection. Sign language is a way of communicating that makes use of nonverbal cues such as facial expressions, body language, and gestures. It can stand in for spoken words and, in some situations, even enhance what people say aloud. People with disabilities now have access to a fully developed sign language. Their method includes an alternative method for warning signals and language with symbols. Check out on the the next image for an improved comprehension on the ways in which individuals with disabilities signs that are used by individuals.

These are the ways that these folks express themselves. Conversely, everyday people convey meaning nonverbally through the use of cultural and universal symbols. Almost everyone on the planet can understand and use a traffic light, making it the most popular universal symbol.

There are also cultural indicators that we use. There are a lot of signals that are culturally significant in India. One example is the universal sound, which is represented by the Indian symbol 'OM' (or 'Ohm' or 'Aum'). Here is an additional illustration. The letter 'V' has multiple interpretations depending on where you are in the globe. Now, let's examine those interpretations:

- USA: It represents a symbol of peace.
- Australia, New Zealand, Ireland and the UK: The symbol is considered to be a sign of rudeness and defiance.

The inquiry "are you an early bird or a night owl?" is often used to inquire about someone's sleeping habits. Here, being an early bird means getting up early and being a night owl means staying up late. When we use these signs and symbols, not only do we communicate more effectively, but they also simplify our lives.

Sign Language: Its Significance

Sign language is very important, as we have already covered. Now let's try to make sense of it. Signs and symbols exist both on a cultural and a universal level. Additionally, we have a highly evolved sign language that is utilized by those with special needs. Consider making an effort to converse with native speakers of languages different than your own. How are you planning to talk to them? Please tell me how to request food, drink, etc. In these kinds of interactions, sign language is crucial. We can simply indicate our desires with our hands, like when we want a glass of water or a bite to eat.

Imagine a scenario where a security agency is searching a location as part of a raid. Because they would rather not be heard, they must employ a system of signs in order to converse with one another, lest it endanger the security guards' lives and their search activities. To convey meaning, they will make use of visual cues. When we hear the siren of an ambulance, fire engine, or police car, what should we do? When the police, firemen, or medical personnel are responding to an emergency, we will hear these auditory indicators. Such vehicles are allowed to pass us when we hear the siren and see the lights flashing on their roof.

Audio visual symbols include both the lights and the sound. In the event of an emergency, they inform us. It facilitates our work and makes our lives easier. In order to communicate effectively in any field, the usage of signs and symbols is crucial.

Proxemics

The field of proxemics analyzes the optimal distance that two people should keep from one another while conversing. Given that the term "proximity" aids in comprehending the closeness of a person in respect to one's relationships, as the name implies. Analysis of the physical people's personal space. We exhibit a connection of some kind when we greet one other silently by shaking hands or embracing. According to Edward T. Hall's research on proxemics, there are four distinct areas of physical proximity between people in an interaction, defined by the nature of the relationships between them. The following are listed:

1) Intimate: With a maximum length of 45 cm (1.5 feet), this is the zone with the closest quarters between individuals. Members of the immediate family, including parents, spouses, and other relatives, all share one room. Close friends and partners also share this place. An embrace, a pat on the back, a grip one side, perched on near each other are a few of the instances where talking about things that are within this realm of talking.

2) Personal: The Individual zone extends from 46 cm to 120 cm (4 feet) on the ground. Considering that the area in question is distributed amongst beloved ones, in the workplace, in the classroom, and a few mutual friends. It has space suggests that the two individuals are somewhat acquainted with one another. As one's degree of familiarity increases, one's proximity to the 46 cm mark decreases and one's distance towards the 120 cm mark increases. Keeping this space in today's world is quite challenging.

Imagine taking the subway at rush hour on your way to or from work or class. Even if they don't know one other, passengers often remain very close to one another. Some individuals may find it upsetting and unpleasant, but in this day and age, it is impossible to totally avoid such circumstances.

3) Social: People-oriented means of expression quite stuffy and bureaucratic. It starts at 12 feet and ends at 3.60 meters, with a distance of 1.21 meters (4 feet). Here we meet new friends, co-workers, acquaintances, and even strangers in an official role, as well as informally at school or the office. Communication in this zone includes asking random people for directions or participating in interviews.

4) Public: It corresponds to discourse that takes place in a public forum, as implied by the text. It begins at 3.61 m (12 feet) and may go all the way to 7.5 m (25 feet), depending on how far one can see or hear. This area of communication is reserved for more official activities, such as classroom lectures, seminars, and training sessions. This communication zone can also include a speech given by a country's head of state on a national holiday, such as Republic Day or Independence Day, or any other event.

These proxemics communication zones are defined in Table 2.

Zones	Distance	Appropriate people/situations
Zone 1 – Intimate	0 - 18 inches	Parents, children, partners, spouse
Zone 2 – Personal	18 inches – 4 feet	Close friends, relatives
Zone 3 – Social	4 feet – 12 feet	Co-workers, social gatherings, worksituations
Zone 4 – Public	12 feet and beyond	Total strangers, actors, importantofficials

Communication Zones in Proxemics (Table 2)

Chronemics

Chronemics was initially used to describe the role of time in communication by researcher Thomas J. Bruneau, who conducted extensive research on non-verbal communication. Put another way, it's the study of how people connect with one another via the passage of time. How we spend our time in the course of our everyday activities reveals a lot about our character. People form unfavourable impressions of people who are chronically late for appointments or who take too long to respond to emails. It could be seen as a sign of excessive enthusiasm if a candidate shows up too early for a job interview. Either monochromic or polychromic time is possible.

1) The Monochronic Time System

Time is seen as money in the popular culture of business, according to Edward T. Hall. For better planning, organization, and administration, this technique divides labor into smaller chunks of time. According to Hall, the American perspective on time is monochronic, meaning that people here treat time like money: precious and preciously should not be squandered.

2) The Polychronic Time System

Performing multiple tasks at once is a hallmark of this time scheme. We see time as a larger unit, rather than discrete activities, and we can accomplish more in the same amount of time if we at the same moment. We can, for instance, While you're typing, answer the phone. Throughout our laptop or while taking notes. Polychronic hyper-focused on the present moment society is particularly in Arab world, South American, the Asian international organizations in this case, time is not split into niche cultural practice those who live in societies where time is measured in terms of ctices, for example.

Things beyond signs and words can be understood through this type of non-verbal communication. We are able to identify the gender and, if known, the voice of a caller within seconds of picking up the phone and hearing them say hello. If the voice is familiar, we can positively identify the individual. Hearing the word "hello" can also give us a clue as to how the individual is feeling. Sadness is obvious to the listener.

Many meanings can be conveyed by the tone and pitch of one's voice. For instance, a teacher's moderate response will have a different effect compared to an appeal to a student who is not responding correctly, as compared to a deaf response.

If the teacher raises her voice, the student may feel humiliated and lose interest in participating in future lessons; but, if the student is chastised, she will attempt to answer appropriately in the future. To gain a better understanding of paralanguage, let's examine the following:

a) Speech Level - The volume of the public speaking audio output needs to be adjusted according to the requirements of the target demographic. Neither too loud nor too quiet is ideal.

b) The Rate of Speech or the tempo at which words are articulated. The pace ought to be just right. It has to be modified according to the audience's skill level.

c) Pause (punctuation)—When used incorrectly, pauses and punctuation can completely alter the intended meaning of a sentence. Some people employ non-fluency sounds like "Ummm" and hesitate too much while they speak, which you must have observed. To be understood by others listening, we must not pause too frequently and refrain from making noises that do not flow naturally.

d) **Word Stress** —Stressing the proper word and syllable is crucial. When we say "climate," for instance, anxiety levels in the initial syllable commands - and -MATE needs to be lacking tension. The effectiveness of any communication process depends on the use of correct word stress.

Haptics

The language of touch is simple to understand. It involves conveying information through physical contact, making it one of the most basic forms of communication.

Babies rely on touch as their primary means of communication with their families. Even an adult can make sense of each alternative using this method of communication. Joining fingers, pecking, sledding etc, this type of communication might include physical gestures like hugging.

Silence

Intriguing as it may seem, one of the most prevalent types of non-verbal communication is simply being silent. Consider a performer who, while onstage, is singing, abruptly stops and is silent. Everyone's attention will be drawn to them, even those who weren't paying attention before. If a defendant does not answer questions about their innocence, the court will likely assume guilt. At funerals, it is respectful to observe a period of quiet. Even in a very noisy classroom, a teacher can get the attention of the kids just by being silent. Quietness reveals a great deal. Refraining from speaking out might have the same effect. Our ability to communicate may be impaired if we remain quiet when prompted to comment or answer a question. To communicate more effectively, we must use our silence wisely.

Meta-Communication

The focus of this kind of transmission is on the recipient's mental processing of the message. Gregory Bateson, an English linguist and anthropologist, popularized the term. He postulated that the speaker-listener relationship, along with all other aspects of the communication process (verbal and nonverbal), governs the meaning of the message. What a speaker says could actually mean something very different. For instance, 'the police station got robbed' has two meanings: first, that someone has plundered the police; second, that the police security is incompetent. How can we trust them to defend the people when they couldn't even defend themselves? Still, there are caveats to this line of thinking. In order to appreciate the irony of the statement, the listener must possess the necessary competencies.

Activity 4

Take a look at these and tell me whether they involve verbal or nonverbal communication.

1) A sales ad for the year.

2) On a board, there is a red plus sign.

3) A mobile phone repairman holds up a placard with images of a screwdriver and a mobile phone.

4) An educator making notes on a whiteboard.

5) Meeting to talk about a project.

6) A bottle with an image of a skull and two bones.

Verbal Communication	Non-verbal communication

3.6 SUMMARY

From what we've gathered, there are essentially two types of communication both oral and body language dialogue. Each kinds of communication are an integral part of our daily life. Both verbal and nonverbal cues are used to enhance communication. There is a vast array of non-verbal behaviours that fall under the umbrella term "non-verbal communication," which does not only comprise signs and symbols. The way we dress, the volume and intonation of our voices, facial expressions, body language, maintaining eye contact, being silent, reaction time, etc., interacts with others and facilitates the formation of a successful interaction between individuals in their personal and geometrical shapes. The present module conveys the significance of a brief notion with relation to different kinds in terms of interaction.

3.7 KEY TERMS

What we call **"verbal communication"** is really just two people expressing themselves via words, whether spoken or written.

Signs, symbols, and other forms of **non-verbal communication** body language, the human language, expressions on the face, body language, and direct eye contact with talk to each other.

Sign language: A language that is expressed through the use of signs and symbols.

Gestures: Movement is what we mean when we talk about gestures.

Body Language: An individual's cranium, hand, or other bodily component to express. A person's non-verbal cues conveyed through their body language.

Proxemics: phrases, behaviour, and idioms to convey meaning. In terms of proxemics, it while maintaining an appropriate distance two individuals ought to maintain eye contact when conversing.

Chronemics is the study of how people interact with time.

3.8 QUESTIONS FOR SELF-EVALUATION

1) How many distinct forms of spoken language exist?

2) How Can We Communicate Without Speaking?

3). How does Kinesis vary from Sign Language?

4) What are proxemics and chronomics?

5) How does Meta-communication vary from Paralanguage?

6) How can one use quiet to convey meaning? Provide instances to illustrate.

UNIT 4

FORM OF COMMUNICATION AT WORKPLACE

OBJECTIVES

After studying this unit you will be able to:

- Understand the concept of communication at workplace;
- Understand types of communication at workplace;
- Appreciate the benefits of effective communication at the workplace.

STRUCTURE

4.1 Introduction
4.2 Formal Communication
4.3 Informal Communication
4.4 Conflict Resolution at Workplace
4.5 Crisis Communication
4.6 Benefits of Effective Communication at Workplace
4.7 Summary
4.8 Keywords
4.9 Self-Assessment Questions

4.1 INTRODUCTION

"Our team has previously discussed that persuasion without using words is essential. Effective communication is key to achieving success on both individual and professional levels."

Likewise, it is critical to the development and success of a company to possess an effective means of communication where the flow of information is readily available and precise. In the modern day, businesses provide their staff with basic communication skills training for new hires and offer seminars where current staff members at all levels can become more effective communicators. Training classes are available for a variety of soft skills, including email writing, competency-based interviewing, and more. The goal of the company's financial and material investments in training is to improve the ability of staff members to interact more efficiently on the job. This results in quicker and more precise communication with a decreased likelihood of setbacks and a reduced spread of misinformation in the workplace. The firm would otherwise lose money due to lost production time caused by inaccurate information transfers or delays.

Cooperation and coordination across different divisions are essential for large organizations. Encouraging staff members to engage effectively helps achieve these goals. Each department's workers communicate with each other to share vital data. They can communicate verbally in person or over the phone, or in writing via various mediums such as letters, memoranda, emails, etc. Although they may speak casually on occasion, the tone of their letters is often official. Both internal and external communications are possible in the workplace. Internal communication refers to interactions between employees of an organization at different or the same levels. External communication describes how a company's employees engage with individuals outside the company. Workers' interactions with external parties can take many forms, including those with clients, potential clients, service providers, contractors, vendors, sponsors, investors, the media, and the public at large.

Letters, emails, memoranda, invoices, account statements, presentations, branding materials, coaching, counselling, taking orders, and more are all part of our job description. The purpose of any kind of workplace communication is to facilitate the effective and timely completion of tasks. Everyone knows their role in the company's reporting structure, which ensures that all company communications flow via the appropriate channels. The significance of both formal and informal forms of workplace communication to personal and professional development is the subject of this unit's teachings.

4.2 FORMAL COMMUNICATION

Communication in an official or formal setting is controlled by established protocols, hierarchies, and channels. Emails, letters, applications, meeting minutes or recordings, corporate video or teleconferencing, etc. are all forms of formal communication. If you want to come across as professional and communicate well, watch your language, tone, pitch, and style. In most companies, there are established rules for how employees should act while interacting with one another, and following these rules involves some thought and effort on the part of workers. Staff members are obligated to adhere to the protocols lest the ongoing tasks encounter any obstruction, delay, or loss due to noncompliance. They risk making a poor image of their work ethic and, in the long run, slowing down their growth cycle if employees do not adhere to appropriate language etiquette and set channels or procedures. There are benefits and drawbacks to using formal language in business. I propose that we examine a few of them:

- One trustworthy method of communication is formal communication. It usually leaves a paper trail that may be followed to find out where it came from. It has additional weight as it is verifiable and may be used as evidence in court.

- Because formal communication must adhere to a rigid line of orders, it moves at a snail's pace. It is expected that employees would use the appropriate channels to communicate with top management and will not circumvent the hierarchy.

- The first lesson on communication is that it can sometimes slow down. People involved may end up spending more time and money than they initially anticipated because of delays. The flow of information is limited and closely monitored, which prevents unnecessary interruptions but also slows everything down.

- The use of appropriate formal communication methods is a safe way to convey information. Only those involved in the legal process or taking part in the deal have access to this data. Unfortunately, not everyone can afford it, whether within the company or from outside, as it is not made public until absolutely necessary. For instance, no one other than the employee and their immediate supervisor can view email correspondence. However, a message outlining broad HR guidelines sent by the HR department is accessible to all company staff. Various types of formal communication are classified according to established channels and organizational structures. These include vertical communication in three different planes.

Vertical Communication

In vertical communication, data is passed up the chain from one level of an organization to another. It has the ability to go horizontally or vertically.

For the sake of clarity, we can further categorize forms of communication as follows:

1) Downward Communication

Among business professionals, this is the language used most frequently while speaking formally. Data is sent from upper to lower echelons of management. The process is hierarchical, beginning with higher-ups and ending with lower-level employees. These include work guidance, policy papers, and important documents that are distributed to employees via email, letters, brochures, pamphlets, etc. They are crucial for the operation of the company's activities, such as production reports, procedure manuals, and announcements.

2) Upward Communication

Here, information flows from the bottom up in a more formal setting like a business. It follows a strict hierarchy, from the most basic to the most advanced levels. From entry-level workers to managers and higher, it often includes requests, job reports, and complaints. It is crucial for management to hear from workers about their opinions, the morale of lower-level staff, their thoughts on new rules and procedures, and any other relevant information. This type of communication occurs in several settings, such as group meetings, reports to supervisors, suggestion or complaint forms dropped off in specific boxes, or requests for redress sent by email, among others.

Looking at table 1, we can see the benefits and drawbacks of vertical communication.

Table 1: Pros and Cons of Top-Down Communication

	Advantages	Disadvantages
1)	It is mostly documented a nd commands a certain level of authority.	It is a slow moving communication and generally involves multiple parties in one transaction.
2)	"It is binding on both the sender and receiver since it typically leaves a paper trail."	The true intention of the sender or receiver can be hidden under the official message it carries.
3)	It has legal validity.	It is less flexible and any change or corrections requires official approval.
4)	Vertical communication is considered official and authentic in nature.	It involves time and money to train people to communicate effectively using appropriate verbal and non-verbal language.

Horizontal and Lateral Communication

Two or more workers on the same level engage in this type of conversation. It is possible that they are in separate or even the same department.

A sales professional chatting with another sales executive, for instance, side to side communication. Someone in charge of sales having conversations with yet another This kind of communication will be used by employees at comparable managerial levels, such as sales managers, production managers, finance managers, etc. The response time is minimal compared to other forms of communication since this type of interaction is taking place between employees at the same level, which makes it somewhat flexible to a vertical position communication. The movement of information in this form of the interaction is horizontal, and it helps teams within the same department or from other departments work together. Horizontal communication, then, is the exchange of ideas and information between workers at the same or comparable levels within an organization.

To		To	
From		From	
Subject		Subject	
Dear Sir/Madam, I am writing this email in response to a job advertisement posted on your website. I meet the essential eligibility criteria and have the desired experience. Please find my CV in the attachment. Kind Regards,		Hi, What's up? It has been a long day. I had so much work. Phew! Hope your day was better. I Hope to have a respite tomorrow. Let's catch up at our regular place. Ping me back Thanks... Have a good day ......Bye bye	

A Gang Plank

Henry Fayol introduced the idea of Gang Plank to improve workplace communication. Another form of lateral or horizontal communication. Employees at the same level or in different departments often communicate with each other for professional reasons in contemporary horizontal communication. Formal authorization is not required for this type of communication. As an example, the VP is the ultimate boss of all the department heads in an organization. Getting in touch with the purchasing manager via the VP is unnecessary if a sales manager want to speak with their counterpart in that department. Gang Plank is quite similar in how it functions when it comes to workplace communication.

In Fayol's terminology, the chain of command is known as the Scalar Chain. According to him, an organization's subordinates can better communicate with their superiors if they are familiar with their roles and responsibilities. Furthermore, the specified hierarchy should always be followed by this scalar sequence of command. However, this command structure can be bypassed in a hurry if necessary, but it is essential to ensure that both immediate supervisors are aware of this bypass.

If F wishes to convey any message, it must traverse each tier of the organizational structure. The typical path for communication is from F to A, then to P, and finally back to F. Going through all the channels would become a tedious and time-consuming task. F, however, can create an 'FP' Gangplank to communicate with P directly in an emergency. Both of them should ensure to alert their direct managers.

"These days, few people in corporate America use this style of horizontal communication. Members of the same level of staff are not required to hold onto letters they exchanged until managers are notified, unless it's absolutely necessary."

Here, we'll go over the benefits and drawbacks of the horizontal or the sideways communication

The Pros and Cons of Horizontal and Lateral Communication (Table 2)

Advantages		Disadvantages
1)	It facilitates coordination between employees of the same or different departments of an organisation. They can share their best practices.	The senior management team may remain uninformed of the proceedings in these departments.
2)	It involves less complexity as compared to vertical communication. The senders and receivers of the message enjoy a certain level of flexibility.	The flexibility in this form of communication may facilitate too much discussion between the employees at the same levels. This may result in confusion and delay in completing assigned tasks
3)	It can expedite communication and save time.	Frequent communication between employees at the same level may facilitate too many informal discourses that may affect the formal policies and procedures at times.

Communication in a diagonal or crosswise plane

This document of business discourse at occupational setting traverses' organizational structures and ranks. Interactions between individuals throughout the company and at all levels of an organizational framework. The persons who speaking in this manner do not originate from the same department nor are they on the same level. The term alludes to dialogue when considering supervisors and employees situated in various departments. For An entry-level sales executive, for instance, can use this kind of communication to have a conversation with a management in the finance department. According to figure 5, these workers come from various departments and are at different levels. Because of the need of employees being able to work efficiently across levels and departments, this type of communication has become an essential component of modern organizations. Other forms of communication include vertical and horizontal communication. Imagine a scenario where a salesperson finds a major mistake made by the marketing team and instead of sending an email to their direct supervisor, goes straight to the marketing team manager to let them know. Since the message won't get hung up in the organizational command chain, it will help fix the mistake faster.

Table 4 lists the benefits and drawbacks of diagonal communication; let's talk about them:

Advantages		Disadvantages
1)	It is the most direct form of formal communication at the workplace.	It affects the chain of commands and breaks the established hierarchical structure in an organisation.
2)	It is one of the fastest and efficient modes of communication at the workplace.	It can bypass the authority of the immediate supervisor who may not have any idea about the actions of his or her subordinate and may be taken by complete surprise if such interactions create any confusion or crisis.
3)	It can help deal with critical situations in the most efficient way.	It can transfer conflicting information if conveyed verbally which may be difficult to verify and hence can create confusion.

The Pros and Cons of Diagonal Communication, Organized in Table 4

4.3 INFORMAL COMMUNICATION

People require to communicate with one another outside of the constraints and hierarchies of formal workplace interactions, which are prevalent while employees are carrying out their obligations for an organization. The First Lesson on Communicating guidelines for formal conversation to foster relationships with others. Therefore, we go above and beyond our professional responsibilities to engage in social interactions with our co-workers. We get to know one other on a more personal level and talk about things other than business when we work together. That part is crucial of our working lives that allows us to escape the confines of sets of predetermined instructions and pathways that characterize human existence at the working environment.

This document means of expression organically derived and consequently, individuals discuss a wide range of subjects in their spare time. More open dialogue on anything from politics to sports to future goals, etc. Oral communication is the norm in this context. Communication between individuals happens more quickly than in a formal setting. The information cannot be verified for its legitimacy because of its intrinsic nature, which prevents it from leaving any paper trace.

A common entry point for employees to initiate informal contact is social interactions. Such communication is often thought of as productive in the workplace since it facilitates team building exercises and allows employees to work together as a cohesive unit. Motivating employees is another responsibility of each other by offering assistance with matters pertaining to employment. Informal communication having open lines of communication may greatly enhance the quality of relationships between work force capable individuals collaborate more effectively as a unit working towards getting there an ordinary goal. This is worth mentioning that It may cause up to the dissemination of false information and rumours due to the prevalence of data lacks control and might cause manufacturing time to be wasted.

These rumour mills have the power to spread rumours that might hurt the company's reputation. Keeping them under control in the beginning is challenging because they swiftly move about. As seen in table 5, there are benefits and drawbacks to informal communication.

Table 5: Pros and Cons of Informal Communication

Advantages		Disadvantages
1)	This is a more flexible form of communication because the channel is multidirectional.	It can cause misunderstanding and spread rumours.
2)	Informal mode of communication at the workplace travels faster as compared to formal communication.	It is difficult to control the flow of information and it can popularize inaccurate data, distort facts, etc.
3)	It can provide feedback about the behaviour of managers to the senior management. A bad or good manager is always at the center of such informal talks and the information reaches the senior management.	These informal communications are orally transferred among people. It does not leave a paper trail. It is impossible to fix the responsibility of such communication at the workplace.
4)	It is a very powerful tool of communication and can impact formal organisational structure.	It can result in the leakage of confidential information. This can affect the functioning of the business process and may result in financial losses.

Types of Informal Communication- Most workplace conversations that take place informally are just innocent chitchat. Conversations like this may happen anywhere: at work, during the lunch break, after hours, and even about personal matters like a co-worker's marriage or divorce. A common way to describe this form of communication is the grapevine. It is a crucial aspect of communication in any company's workplace. Grapevine is a two-way street of information. Relationships between individuals and accepted social practices, rather than codified policies, control its operation. Different orientations of this kind of communication are possible. Based on his research into this method of dissemination, Professor Keith Davis (1979) concluded that "the grapevine is a natural part of a company's total communication system...it is a significant force within the work group, helping to build teamwork, motivate people, and create a corporate identity." As seen in figure 6, he divided it into the following groups.

It entails passing on knowledge from one person in a group or line to another. As an example, let's say that member A shares certain data with member B. Then, the knowledge is passed on from member B to member C, who in turn passes it on to member D, and so on.

Gossip Chain

One way to look at this kind of casual conversation is as a means of gathering and relaying information to everyone in a group. Just one man is critical spot along the distribution of relevant data. He or she remains centred around communication of data. Member A can share data with member B, for instance, class B, class "C," a constituent D, and hence on.

"Refer to Figure 8 to better understand the concepts."In this kind of casual conversation, person A is pivotal to the flow of information. In addition to actively seeking out information, s/he also passes it to other members. None of the other members communicate with one another in a direct manner.

Probability Chain

The knowledge is passed down from one person to another at random in this sort of grapevine communication. They don't pick someone to take part. There is no discernible structure or sequence to the data's movement. In this case, Member A can share data with Members B, D, I, etc. Then, in a similar way, those members can transmit the identical data. To better grasp its operation,

It is clear that the data is being sent around among the participants at random. It is not focused on transmitting information from a single member and does not adhere to any particular sequence or chain, unlike Gossip Chain or Single Strand Chain. Data travels quicker and with less restriction. It also seems to operate at random according to the rule of chance and doesn't always engage all members.

Cluster Chain

Members who have access to the message choose new recipients, and the process continues iteratively. A group of people conversing and passing the word on to new members is the way the data travels. As an illustration, let's say that A shares certain knowledge with B and C. Here, A is communicating with B and C, who are the intended recipients of the communication. After that, the incoming members act as messengers, passing the message on to the new recipients.

The receiver would then forward the message to yet another group of recipients once it has been transmitted by person A. Here, A communicates with B, C, D, and F by passing along the data. After that, it goes from F to G, who re-delivers it to H, I, and J. After receiving information from one sender, the receiver always assumes the function of the sender.

4.4 CONFLICTS RESOLUTION AT WORKPLACE

"Communication in the office is not solely about building rapport and being kind. Individuals from various generations and educational backgrounds collaborate within an organization. "Their backgrounds, experiences, and personalities are all unique, and
life's experiences. As a result, they can end themselves in a contentious scenario due to their divergent opinions. In the long run, these conflict situations have the potential to grow into major crises causing problems that, if left unchecked, might cripple company operations. When conflicts emerge, whether they are based on professional or personal disagreements, managers need to act professionally and employ effective techniques to resolve them in a way that everyone is happy. When resolving conflicts in a fair manner, they can employ the following tactics:

a) Active listening

A crucial component of effective communication is listening attentively maturing into a decent conveying ideas. The manager or peer mediating the disagreement has to listen attentively so they can grasp the problem at hand. It is important to listen carefully and attentively to both sides. The mediator's job is to sit quietly and listen to both sides' arguments. As a result, two potential advantages "Everyone involved in the dispute will have an opportunity to express their displeasure, and the mediator can potentially help them come to an agreement. Addressing competing viewpoints can foster a tranquil environment and lead to a final decision beneficial to both parties. However, a solution cannot be achieved without attentive listening."

b) Set Goals

The mediator must inspire the parties to come to the meeting with the belief that they can reach a settlement. They need to pay close attention to one another and come up with ideas for areas of agreement. Disagreement is healthy, however while resolving a disagreement, everyone involved should remember that they are in this together to find a solution to the problem, not against one other.

c) Stay Professional

Workplace conflicts can emerge from animosity amongst co-workers at the same or different levels. Issues stemming from individual differences have the potential to heighten the emotional reaction and exacerbate the conflict scenario. Resolving a quarrel requires all sides to maintain composure and control their emotional reactions. Being cool and collected is going to help. Strong professional etiquette requires one to remain cool and collected under pressure. Resolving the disagreement gets simpler when one can approach it with a clearer head.

d) Stay Neutral

To successfully resolve a problem, this is a crucial tactic. The disputing parties are more likely to accept a neutral mediator if they are participating in the mediation process. To show that s/he is not taking sides, the mediator must listen carefully to each side and then summarize the main points of contention. If everyone participating in the mediation views the mediator as impartial, the parties are more inclined to accept the mediator's recommended solution. Conversely, the settlement of the dispute is more likely to be unsuccessful if the mediator is seen of as prejudiced.

e) Facts Checking

When trying to resolve a disagreement, it is crucial to verify information. The mediator must ascertain all relevant information before making a determination. Verifying all information and listening to other points of view is crucial. The best way for the mediator to get to the bottom of a dispute is to give each side a chance to tell their narrative. If you're trying to come up with a solution, it may be useful. To determine the true state of affairs and offer a solution that can be agreed upon by everyone involved, a comprehensive investigation is necessary. In order to ensure that the offered solution is effective, the mediator must pay close attention to all of the information given during the dispute resolution process.

4.5 CRISIS COMMUNICATION

In the event of an emergency, this form of workplace communication focuses on safeguarding the organization and its employees. At both the organizational and individual levels, it addresses the danger that may devastate the whole company. Data security breaches, product recalls, insolvency, and other similar events necessitate crisis communication at the organizational level. On an employee level, it might address issues like sexual harassment, burns, and other accidents.

"A brief overview of working with co-workers is to ensure that all conversations run smoothly and that the communication system is capable of efficiently handling emergency scenarios. "For instance, you've probably heard of or participated in a company's fire drills. Employees will be prepared to respond appropriately in the event of a fire on the job site thanks to these drills. It is our PR specialists doing duties for a business. Those people are professionals have the necessary skills to convey ideas clearly in an event that can incorporates news outlets to safeguard the company's credibility.

For an organization to run smoothly, communication is key. There is no system in place for stakeholders to communicate during crises, and they cannot afford to take any chances. An organization can't have successful crisis communication without a solid communication plan and enough staff training. In the event of a financial catastrophe, natural calamity, human injury, etc., the organizations will be better prepared.

4.6 BENEFITS OF EFFECTIVE COMMUNICATION AT WORKPLACE

1) Having fruitful conversations requires a strong work ethic and strong communication abilities with other staff members."

2) It promotes a positive work environment where employees trust one another. They believe in the company's purpose, objectives, and future plans.

(3) "It has the potential to foster a conducive social setting. In such an environment, individuals tend to perform at a higher quality when they develop friendships with co-workers. They can then encourage one another."

4) Employees are able to bond via the power of good communication, leadership, and administration.

5) "Maintaining explicit and easily understood directions through communication is essential. When workers comprehend policies, processes, and instructions well, their satisfaction levels increase, leading to happier employees."

6) Cohesive teams are the result of good communication. The staff will not only cooperate, but will also support one another in reaching the objectives.

7) It will facilitate the swift resolution of disputes. When individuals unite for a shared goal, conflict is inevitable. In earlier parts of this subject, we covered how good communication may aid in resolving conflicts.

8) It will encourage a secure setting on the job. When a business makes it clear that it cares about its workers' well-being and is ready to handle medical or natural disasters, workers know they can trust the organization to keep them safe on the job.

Activity 2

Take a look at the following examples of workplace communication and label them as either formal or informal.

1) A personal journal entry made by an employee.

2) A meeting of the staff in the break room to talk business.

3) A meeting room debate over an evaluation.

4) An email-based procedure for resolving disputes.

5) A corporate email informing a co-worker of weekend plans.

6) A policy booklet outlining incentives, handed out by the HR manager.

7) A group of co-workers spoke about taking time off to celebrate a colleague's wedding.

Formal Communication at Workplace	Informal Communication at Workplace

4.7 SUMMARY

We understand the value of clear and concise communication in the business world. There are two main types of workplace communication: formal and informal. Both official and informal forms of communication are critical to the development and prosperity of any business and its workers. A correct line of command is followed in formal communications, which are authoritarian in character. Conversely, there is no predetermined order of command in informal conversations; rather, they are democratic in character. To reach its full potential, a company must master the art of formal and informal communication. It is critical for a company to teach its workers how to communicate well so that they can accomplish their daily tasks and the company's objectives.

4.8 KEY TERMS

- For official reasons, it is necessary to transmit information over a predetermined and authorized me00dia. This type of communication is known as **formal communication**.

- Formal information goes from superiors to subordinates and vice versa in **vertical communication.**

- A brief overview of **Horizontal communication** is a type of business-related discourse in which different parts of an organisation share and receive information from one another.

- A type of formal communication known as **"diagonal" or "crosswise" communication** occurs when workers from various departments or divisions of an organization communicate information with one another.

- A company's **"grapevine"** is the unofficial channel by which word is passed around amongst employees. It goes by another name: **conversation informally**.

- The goal of **conflict resolution** is to help employees resolve disagreements that arise between different departments or even different companies.

- The term **"crisis communication"** describes the methods used to address the most serious dangers that a company may   encounter.

4.9 SELF-ASSESSMENT QUESTIONS

1) How do you define "formal communication" in the business world?

2) What is the difference between diagonal communication and gang plank?

3) Outline the benefits and drawbacks of omitting a defined organizational structure for workplace communication?

4) In a business setting, what does it mean to communicate informally?

5) What advantages can a grapevine offer to a business? What does it mean to resolve conflicts effectively? Give an example to illustrate your point.

CASE STUDY

CASE STUDY -1

In a global tech firm headquartered in Silicon Valley, an American project manager named Sarah leads a diverse team of software engineers working on a ground breaking artificial intelligence project. Sarah's team comprises members from India, Japan, and Germany, reflecting the company's commitment to diversity and innovation. However, despite their shared goal of creating cutting-edge technology, cultural differences often lead to communication challenges.

During a virtual meeting to discuss the project's progress, Sarah enthusiastically presents a new strategy to streamline the development process and improve efficiency. She expects her team to provide feedback and suggestions for improvement. However, as Sarah outlines her proposal, she notices that her team members seem hesitant to speak up. Their responses are brief, and some even nod in agreement without offering any additional insights.

Assuming that her team is on board with the proposed strategy, Sarah concludes the meeting and moves forward with the implementation plan. However, over the following weeks, she notices a lack of enthusiasm and engagement from her team. Deadlines are missed, and productivity begins to decline. Concerned about the project's trajectory, Sarah decides to schedule individual meetings with her team members to address their concerns.

During these one-on-one meetings, Sarah learns that her team members from India, Japan, and Germany were uncomfortable with the proposed strategy but hesitated to express their reservations openly. In their respective cultures, direct confrontation and disagreement with authority figures are often avoided to maintain harmony and respect. Instead of voicing their concerns directly, the team members chose to remain silent or provide vague responses during the virtual meeting.

Reflecting on the situation, Sarah realizes that she failed to consider the cultural nuances of her team members' communication styles. In the American workplace culture, open and assertive communication is often encouraged, but this approach may not align with the communication norms of other cultures. Moving forward, Sarah commits to fostering a more inclusive and culturally sensitive work environment. She encourages her team members to express their opinions and concerns openly, regardless of cultural differences, and implements regular check-ins to ensure that everyone feels heard and valued.

CASE STUDY -2

In the heart of New York City, a prestigious multinational hotel chain prides itself on delivering exceptional customer service to guests from around the world. As part of its commitment to diversity, the hotel hires Miguel, a customer service representative from Spain, to join its front desk team. Miguel is fluent in English and possesses excellent interpersonal skills, making him an ideal candidate for the role. However, despite his language proficiency, Miguel's strong Spanish accent becomes a source of frustration for some guests.

On several occasions, guests have difficulty understanding Miguel over the phone when making reservations or requesting assistance. Despite his best efforts to communicate clearly, his accent often leads to misunderstandings and confusion. Some guests become impatient or frustrated, resulting in negative reviews and complaints about the hotel's customer service standards.

Recognizing the impact of the language barrier on customer satisfaction, the hotel's management team decides to take proactive measures to address the issue. They enroll Miguel in accent reduction training to help him improve his pronunciation and enunciation. Additionally, the hotel implements a system for clearer communication, such as providing scripts for common interactions or offering bilingual support for guests who prefer to communicate in their native language.

Through dedicated practice and training, Miguel gradually improves his accent and communication skills, making it easier for guests to understand him over the phone. The hotel receives fewer complaints about language barriers, and Miguel's confidence in his abilities grows as he becomes more proficient in delivering exceptional customer service.

CASE STUDY -3

Scenario: In a bustling marketing agency with offices in both the United States and China, cross-cultural collaboration is essential for success. However, despite their shared passion for creativity and innovation, communication challenges often arise between team members from different cultural backgrounds.

During a recent email exchange discussing a new marketing campaign, tensions flare as misinterpretations and misunderstandings abound. The American team members, known for their direct and assertive communication style, provide feedback that is perceived as overly critical and blunt by their Chinese counterparts. In contrast, the Chinese team members' responses are viewed as evasive and lacking in substance by their American colleagues.

As the email chain continues, frustration mounts on both sides, leading to a breakdown in communication and a decline in productivity. Recognizing the need to address the issue before it escalates further, the agency's leadership team schedules a series of cross-cultural communication workshops for all staff members.

During these workshops, employees learn about the cultural differences in communication styles between the U.S. and China. They discuss strategies for bridging these differences and fostering effective collaboration, such as being mindful of language choices, providing context for feedback, and seeking clarification when needed.

Armed with a deeper understanding of each other's communication preferences and cultural norms, the marketing agency's teams navigate future projects with greater empathy and respect. By embracing diversity and promoting cross-cultural understanding, they enhance their ability to collaborate effectively and achieve shared goals.

CASE STUDY -4

Scenario: In the competitive world of pharmaceutical research and development, timely decision-making is critical for success. However, in a multinational pharmaceutical company with offices in Brazil and Sweden, cultural differences in power distance create challenges during the decision-making process.

During a video conference to discuss the development of a new drug, tensions arise as the Swedish team expresses concerns about the safety of the drug's ingredients. They suggest delaying the launch for further testing to ensure regulatory compliance and mitigate potential risks. However, their Brazilian counterparts, accustomed to a hierarchical organizational structure where authority figures are respected and decisions are rarely challenged, defer to the authority of the senior manager leading the project.

Despite their reservations, the Brazilian team members hesitate to voice their concerns openly, fearing repercussions or undermining the authority of their superiors. As a result, the decision to proceed with the drug's launch as planned is made without fully addressing the Swedish team's valid concerns.

In the aftermath of the decision, tensions simmer between the Swedish and Brazilian teams, eroding trust and collaboration. Recognizing the need to bridge the cultural gap and foster a more inclusive decision-making process, the company's leadership team implements training programs on cross-cultural communication and leadership.

Through these programs, employees learn about the concept of power distance and its impact on decision making in different cultural contexts. They discuss strategies for promoting transparency, encouraging open dialogue, and empowering team members to voice their opinions and concerns without fear of retribution.

CASE STUDY -5

In the fast-paced world of international business negotiations, nonverbal communication cues play a crucial role in shaping perceptions and outcomes. However, in a recent negotiation between an Australian company and a Japanese firm, cultural differences in nonverbal communication lead to a breakdown in communication and a failed partnership.

During the negotiation meeting, the Australian managers maintain steady eye contact and speak assertively to convey confidence and credibility. However, their Japanese counterparts interpret these behaviours as confrontational and arrogant, causing tension and discomfort in the room. As the negotiation progresses, misinterpretations and misunderstandings abound, making it difficult for both parties to find common ground.

Despite their best efforts to salvage the partnership, the negotiation ends in deadlock, leaving both the Australian company and the Japanese firm disappointed and frustrated. Reflecting on the experience, the Australian managers recognize the need to develop a deeper understanding of cultural differences in nonverbal communication.

They enroll in cross-cultural communication training programs to learn about the importance of context, gestures, and body language in different cultural contexts. They discover that in Japanese culture, maintaining eye contact can be perceived as intrusive or aggressive, while silence is often used as a means of conveying respect or disagreement.

Armed with this newfound knowledge, the Australian managers approach future negotiations with greater sensitivity and cultural awareness. They adapt their communication style to align with the expectations and preferences of their Japanese counterparts, fostering a more collaborative and mutually beneficial relationship.

By embracing cultural diversity and recognizing the impact of nonverbal communication cues, the Australian company strengthens its global partnerships and expands its presence in the international market.

A multinational fashion retailer, with headquarters in London and regional offices in Tokyo and Mumbai, faces a challenge in decision-making due to cultural differences. The company is planning to launch a new clothing line targeting the youth market, and the marketing team needs to decide on the design elements and advertising strategy.

During the brainstorming session, the London-based team presents bold and edgy design concepts, emphasizing individuality and self-expression. However, the Tokyo team prefers designs that are more subtle and minimalist, reflecting Japanese aesthetics and cultural values. Meanwhile, the Mumbai team advocates for vibrant colors and intricate patterns inspired by traditional Indian textiles.

As the discussions unfold, it becomes clear that each team's preferences are influenced by their cultural backgrounds and market insights. Recognizing the importance of diversity in decision-making, the company's leadership decides to leverage the strengths of each team by incorporating elements from all three proposals into the final product.

The resulting clothing line combines elements of British urban street-wear, Japanese minimalism, and Indian craftsmanship, appealing to a diverse range of customers globally. By embracing cultural diversity and fostering collaboration across teams, the company not only enhances its product offerings but also strengthens its brand identity as a culturally inclusive fashion retailer.

CASE STUDY 6

Scenario: A software development company, with offices in San Francisco and Bangalore, experiences a conflict between team members from the two locations. The conflict arises during a project meeting when the San Francisco-based team criticizes the quality of code produced by their counterparts in Bangalore, citing frequent bugs and delays in delivery.

The Bangalore team feels unfairly targeted and believes that their San Francisco colleagues are not considering the challenges they face, such as language barriers and differences in time zones. Tensions escalate as both teams become defensive, blaming each other for the project's setbacks.

Recognizing the need for conflict resolution, the company's leadership arranges a series of mediation sessions facilitated by a trained mediator with expertise in cross-cultural communication. During these sessions, team members from both locations have the opportunity to express their perspectives and concerns in a safe and supportive environment.

Through active listening and constructive dialogue, the teams identify common goals and explore ways to address their differences collaboratively. They agree to implement a more structured communication process, including regular video conferences and written documentation of project requirements and feedback.

As a result of the mediation process, trust and understanding between the San Francisco and Bangalore teams improve significantly. They work together more effectively, leveraging their complementary skills and perspectives to deliver high-quality software products on time and within budget.

CASE STUDY 7

Scenario: A luxury hotel chain expands its operations to the Middle East, opening a new flagship property in Dubai. As part of its commitment to providing exceptional customer service, the hotel hires staff from diverse cultural backgrounds to cater to the needs of its international clientele.

During a training session for front desk staff, the hotel's management emphasizes the importance of cultural sensitivity in customer interactions. They provide guidance on greeting guests respectfully, addressing cultural differences in communication styles, and adapting service delivery to meet the preferences of each guest.

One day, a guest from Japan checks into the hotel and expresses dissatisfaction with the room assigned to him, citing cultural preferences for certain amenities and room layouts. The front desk staff, trained in cultural sensitivity, listens attentively to the guest's concerns and offers alternative accommodation options that better align with his preferences.

Impressed by the hotel's responsiveness and attention to detail, the guest's initial dissatisfaction turns into delight as he enjoys a comfortable and enjoyable stay. He praises the hotel's commitment to understanding and accommodating the needs of its diverse clientele, resulting in positive word-of-mouth referrals and repeat business.

By prioritizing cultural sensitivity in customer service, the luxury hotel chain not only enhances the guest experience but also strengthens its reputation as a welcoming and inclusive destination for travelers from around the world.

CASE STUDY 8

A leading hospitality chain was facing challenges with customer satisfaction and retention due to poor communication skills among its customer service representatives. Despite the company's commitment to providing exceptional service, customers often reported feeling frustrated and undervalued when interacting with frontline staff. Recognizing the critical role that effective communication plays in delivering a positive customer experience, the company decided to invest in a comprehensive customer service communication training program for its employees.

The customer service communication training program focused on various aspects of communication, including active listening, empathy, and problem-solving. Employees were taught how to greet customers warmly, listen attentively to their needs and concerns, and communicate clearly and effectively to address any issues or inquiries. Role-playing exercises and simulations were used to provide practical examples and opportunities for employees to practice their communication skills in realistic scenarios.

One of the key objectives of the training program was to empower employees to take ownership of customer interactions and ensure that every customer felt valued and appreciated. Employees were encouraged to go above and beyond to exceed customer expectations and create memorable experiences that would inspire loyalty and repeat business.

As a result of the customer service communication training initiative, significant improvements were observed in customer satisfaction and retention. Customers reported feeling more satisfied and appreciated when interacting with frontline staff, leading to increased loyalty and positive word-of-mouth referrals. Moreover, the company saw a reduction in customer complaints and escalations, as employees became more adept at addressing issues proactively and resolving them to the customer.

CASE STUDY 9

Scenario: A global consulting firm, with offices in New York, London, and Singapore, faces a challenge in managing conflicts within its multicultural project teams. During a recent client engagement, tensions arise between team members from different locations over the allocation of tasks and responsibilities.

The New York team, known for its assertive and results-oriented approach, takes the lead in driving the project forward, often making decisions without consulting their counterparts in London and Singapore. Feeling marginalized and undervalued, the London and Singapore teams become increasingly frustrated, leading to communication breakdowns and missed deadlines.

Recognizing the need to address the conflict before it escalates further, the project manager, based in New York, schedules a series of team-building workshops and conflict resolution sessions. During these sessions, team members have the opportunity to share their perspectives and concerns openly, facilitated by a trained mediator with expertise in cross-cultural communication.

Through guided exercises and role-playing scenarios, team members develop a deeper understanding of each other's communication styles, working preferences, and cultural backgrounds. They identify common goals and establish clear guidelines for collaboration, including regular check-ins, transparent decision-making processes, and mutual respect for each other's expertise and contributions.

As a result of the conflict resolution process, trust and camaraderie among team members strengthen significantly. They work together more cohesively, leveraging their diverse skills and perspectives to deliver outstanding results for their clients. By prioritizing open communication and cultural sensitivity, the consulting firm not only resolves conflicts effectively but also fosters a more inclusive and collaborative work environment.

CASE STUDY 10

An international technology start up, with team members hailing from the United States, China, and India, faces a leadership challenge as it scales its operations and expands into new markets. The company's CEO, based in Silicon Valley, recognizes the importance of cultural intelligence in leading diverse teams effectively.

During a leadership retreat, the CEO facilitates a series of workshops and discussions on cross-cultural communication, leadership styles, and conflict resolution. Team members share their experiences and insights, highlighting the unique cultural perspectives they bring to the table and the challenges they face in collaborating across borders.

Inspired by the discussions, the CEO commits to fostering a culture of inclusivity and empowerment within the organization. They implement strategies to ensure that all team members have equal opportunities to contribute and grow, regardless of their cultural background or geographical location.

The CEO leads by example, demonstrating cultural sensitivity and humility in their interactions with team members from different cultures. They actively seek feedback and input from all team members, encourage open dialogue and collaboration, and celebrate the diversity of perspectives and ideas that drive innovation and success.

As a result of the CEO's leadership and commitment to cultural intelligence, the technology start up thrives in the global marketplace, attracting top talent from around the world and forging strong partnerships with clients and stakeholders. By prioritizing diversity and inclusion at every level of the organization, the company achieves sustainable growth and creates a workplace where everyone feels valued, respected, and empowered to succeed.